Assessment

Evidence-based Teaching
for Enquiring Teachers

Assessment

Evidence-based Teaching
for Enquiring Teachers

Chris Atherton

First published in 2018 by Critical Publishing Ltd

British Library Cataloguing in Publication Data

A CIP record for this book is available from the British Library

ISBN: 9781912096497

This book is also available in the following e-book formats:

MOBI ISBN: 9781912096480
EPUB ISBN: 9781912096473
Adobe e-book ISBN: 9781912096466

Cover design by Out of House Limited
Text design by Out of House Limited
Project management by Out of House Publishing Solutions
Printed and bound in Great Britain by Bell & Bain, Glasgow

Critical Publishing
3 Connaught Road
St Albans
AL3 5RX

 www.criticalpublishing.com

For orders and details of our bulk discounts please go to our website or contact our distributor NBN International by telephoning 01752 202301 or emailing orders@nbninternational.com.

Contents

Meet the series editor

Val Poultney

Val Poultney is a senior lecturer at the University of Derby. She teaches on initial teacher education and postgraduate programmes. Her research interests include school leadership and school governance with a particular focus on how to develop leadership to support teachers as researchers.

Meet the author

Chris Atherton

Chris Atherton is an English teacher, head of department and research lead at Sir John Deane's Sixth Form College in the North West of England. His personal academic interests are cultural evolution, linguistics and cognitive science.

Foreword

It is a great pleasure to introduce this new book by Chris Atherton entitled *Assessment*, which is the first book in the series 'Evidence-based Teaching for Enquiring Teachers'. Chris, who is head of department and research lead at Sir John Deane's Sixth Form College in the North West of England, was in part influenced by Daisy Christodolou's book *Making Good Progress?* Her work sought to offer a link between formative assessment and cognitive science. Practitioners will be acquainted with the two variants of assessment: Assessment *of* Learning and Assessment *for* Learning (AfL). While the former has a focus on grading and reporting (often referred to as summative assessment), the latter draws more heavily on theoretical ideas being operationalised in the classroom and is a form of formative assessment that seeks to move learning along (Black and Wiliam, 1998). The aim of Chris' book is to draw together evidence generated from academic research about assessment and present it in a way that allows practitioners to look for and critically interpret the evidence base to inform their own planning and teaching. After all, practitioners are best placed to understand their students' learning, where they are in that learning journey, where they need to go and the best course of action to get them there.

The decentralisation of the education landscape has meant that schools now seek different alliances not just with other schools but also with universities, private providers and businesses, to name but a few. The resurgence of teachers as researchers (Stenhouse, 1975) inquiring into their own practice and generating their own knowledge has seen a shift in the ways in which teachers are approaching their own learning and professional development. There has been a proliferation of bodies such as ResearchED (https://researched.org.uk/), the Educational Endowment Foundation (https://educationendowmentfoundation.org.uk/) and the Mapping Educational Specialist knowHow webpages known as the MESH guides (www.meshguides.org/mesh-guides/), all of which seek to close the gap between academic research on assessment and how those outcomes might be put into practice in schools. There is also a government push for teachers to be a bigger part of school-based reform, so it is important for teachers to be able to generate and evaluate evidence that will support not only assessment criteria but the learning needs of all their students.

In the spirit of encouraging practitioners to engage in research and enquiry, this book focuses on helping teachers to critically engage with a range of issues around assessment and offers them the opportunity to reflect on their own practice. Complex research issues are broken down and summarised in ways that are easily accessible to busy practitioners while offering a broad

range of follow-up readings for those interested in pursuing topics in more depth. The principles behind the
efficacy of AfL are explained, drawing upon the evidence bases and how these ideas can be practically implemented in the classroom setting with learners.

It is my belief that Chris' book will inspire colleagues in schools and universities to take a fresh look at AfL through the evidence-informed lens. It aims to offer an alternative way of thinking about assessment strategies that are applicable to all phases of schooling. The format is accessible and practical and of particular interest to a range of professionals, including Initial Teacher Education students, newly qualified and experienced practitioners alike.

Val Poultney, series editor
Senior Lecturer in Education, University of Derby

References

Black, P and Wiliam, D (1998) Inside the Black Box: Raising Standards Through Classroom Assessment. *Phi Delta Kappan*, 80: 139–48.

Stenhouse, L (1975) *An Introduction to Research and Development*. London: Heinemann.

Chapter 1
Introduction

1.1 Chapter overview

This chapter will outline:

1.2   what assessment is;

1.3   the assessment debate;

1.4   why it is important to take an evidence-based approach;

1.5   the topics covered by this book.

1.2 What is assessment?

Assessment is a fundamental component of learning. It is *'a process of gathering information for the purpose of making judgments about a current state of affairs'* (Pellegrino, 2002, p 48). It serves as a tool both for measuring achievement and driving the learning process. When those working in education use the term, they are also describing a strand of pedagogy with its own specific theory, evidence and practice. In recent years, research has increasingly shown that assessment is one of the most powerful tools available for improving standards in education.

Types of assessment

The most important distinction is the distinction between *formative* and *summative* assessment.

Table 1a Formative and summative assessment

Summative assessment	Assessment in the traditional sense, where you measure a student's success against criteria to assign success or failure at the the end of the learning process.
Formative assessment	The use of assessment as a tool for learning during the learning process. Assessment is used to evaluate comprehension and learning, thereby facilitating better teaching.

The basic principle of formative assessment is that through assessing performance throughout the learning process (not just at the end), we can generate better conditions for learning. This is achieved either through offering feedback, or through adapting later learning to better fit the needs of the student. As Stiggins (2002, p 759) explains:

once-a-year tests are incapable of providing teachers with the moment-to-moment and day-to-day information about student achievement that they need to make crucial instructional decisions. Teachers must rely on classroom assessment to do this.

The line between summative and formative assessment can often feel very subjective. Cowie and Bell (1999, p 105) try to explain the distinction by describing formative assessment as '*the process used by teachers and students to recognize and respond to student learning in order to enhance that learning, during the learning*'. Formative assessment is an ongoing process and a mode of practice, whereas summative assessment is infrequent and final.

Assessment for Learning

One common synonym that you may encounter is Assessment for Learning (AfL), a term which has come to replace formative assessment in some recent policy discussions. This term was probably coined by Scriven (1967) but has been popularised through the work of Stiggins (2002; 2005). This term arose out of the need to try to clarify a particular definition of formative assessment, one which '*differs from assessment designed primarily to serve the purposes of accountability, or of ranking, or of certifying competence*' (Black et al, 2004, p 10). As assessment is also often used for accountability purposes, the fear was that unless a distinction was made between formative assessment in the wider sense and AfL, teachers may not focus on the right version. The value of this distinction is still questioned (Wiliam, 2016, p 105) as it has both muddied the waters further, and also because it fails to capture all possible dimensions of formative assessment. This debate over the use of this term, while interesting, is not resolved, so this book will adopt the term *formative assessment* for all manifestations of the concept, unless it is exclusively tackling research in which AfL is discussed in its narrow sense.

1.3 The assessment debate

For those seeking to raise standards in education, improving learning through better or more appropriate assessment is a very attractive concept. Formative assessment has developed a reputation for being low-cost, highly effective and scalable. It is not surprising that it has been made a central plank of education reform in the UK. At least one proponent has dubbed it '*transformative assessment*' (Popham, 2008, 2011). Proponents of formative assessment have been working with policymakers and school leaders for over a decade now, leading to what Baird et al (2014, p 4) call the *'rise of assessment'*. This rise is not without controversy, and some have been critical of the way in which it has been associated with a neoliberal model of education, where learning is quantified to make it subject to market forces (Hursh, 2007; Pratt, 2016). Given this controversy, and that formative assessment is now embedded as policy at a local and national level, it is more important than ever to reflect critically on the evidence which underpins it.

One of the key issues is the inherent difficulty in defining what we mean by improving learning through assessment. There is considerable evidence of powerful effects in relation to formative assessment techniques, but we do not have a robust and mutually understood definition of what formative assessment is. Even Dylan Wiliam who, alongside Paul Black, is considered by many to be the original intellectual force behind formative assessment, offers the confounding assertion that '*formative assessment is not a thing*' (Wiliam, 2016, p 106). This deliberately provocative assertion is not meant to undermine the idea, but to illustrate the difficulty in defining formative assessment as separate from assessment in a wider sense. The most recent iteration of the idea has defined formative assessment as the bridge between teaching and learning. In this definition, rather than being a set of universal strategies, it manifests differently in different academic environments. The debate has shifted from *can formative assessment improve learning?* to *how do I get it to work in my classroom?*

This book is designed to examine and evaluate the evidence on both sides of the assessment debate for teachers working in all sectors of the education system. It will explore the tension between universal and specific claims about assessment and the role that wider structures (school culture, Continuing Professional Development (CPD), national policies) play in classroom assessment. In doing so, it will show how an evidence-based approach is the best way to find answers to these controversies. This book aims to give you a tour of the evidence base on which those claims have been made, highlighting the areas of strength and weakness and evaluating the validity of the claims made.

1.4 Why take an evidence-based approach to assessment?

In recent years, a diverse group of researchers, educational leaders and teachers have advocated for evidence-based pedagogies. These advocates have emerged from academic communities, government, charities and professional networks on social media. In the process, they have built government-funded institutions like the Education Endowment Foundation, resource banks for teachers, and teacher-organised conferences like ResearchED (whose slogan is *'working out what works'*). This group is, at best, informally organised and understood, and has emerged in parallel with government advocacy evidence-based approaches to teacher training (Carter, 2015). At present, research-based pedagogies are in the ascendance, largely because they offer something that previous initiatives have never done – empirical evidence of their own effectiveness. However, this does come with significant new challenges for teachers. Research evidence is subject to much higher demands of proof than previous approaches, and the profession itself is generally untrained in using and critically reading research. In addition, all the old pressures on assessment remain, including Ofsted expectations and individual school cultures. There is still much work to be done on the intersection between academic research and schools themselves, particularly in the development of school–university partnerships. The path of evidence into the classroom has been neither smooth, nor universally successful. Changing the status quo is a challenge that the whole profession must undertake, and Goldacre (2013) has suggested that education is experiencing something like the paradigm shift which took place in medicine in the early twentieth century.

This book is a guided tour through the evidence on assessment from a teacher's perspective, but with the academic rigour to engage with the evidence in a way that few teachers are trained to do. If you've been asked to 'use assessment better' by a manager, or a university tutor, this book will help you understand what that might actually mean. This book is described as *evidence-based* because:

- it presents the evidence on assessment in the classroom;
- it only evaluates approaches to assessment that have an evidence base to suggest their efficacy, and maintains scepticism towards those that do not.

Making assessment work is not a trivial issue. In a recent Department for Education survey of teacher workload, teachers identified marking, planning and data management as the three biggest challenges that they face (Higton et al, 2017). All three of these are directly related to how we conduct assessment, and there is therefore a moral duty for teacher and leaders alike to reflect upon the efficacy of different assessment approaches. Wasting time on assessment that doesn't work causes excess workload for teachers and has a negative impact on student achievement. Similarly, effective assessment interventions can lead to measurable improvements in summative assessment outcomes, and learning efficiency.

What does good research look like?

The evidence available to teachers is often patchy and of a mixed quality, which makes it even more critical that teachers know what good research looks like. Coe (2012) argues that there are six characteristics of effective educational research (see Table 1b).

Table 1b Criteria for valid educational research, adapted from Coe (2012, p 10)

Critical	It questions claims, methods and professional assumptions.
Systemic	It is deliberate and planned, and follows through on lines of enquiry in a logical way.
Transparent	All the aspects of value to making an assessment, such as the aims, methodology, data etc, are available to those seeking to evaluate the claims being made.
Evidential	Claims are based on evidence and data, not intuition or common-sense readings.
Theoretical	Research is both guided by theory, and tests and provides evidence for and against theories.
Original	It aims to add to existing knowledge.

This book will summarise the available evidence, and discuss its implications for professional practice. The focus will be on research which meets these six criteria, and where relevant, the strengths and limitations of individual pieces of research will be discussed.

There has been an explosion of other extremely useful sources of information over the past few years, including teacher blogs and social media. While these are often excellent informal sources of information for teachers, they will not be discussed in this book as its focus is on peer-reviewed research. The sources used in this book are all peer-reviewed and have been chosen for their robust academic credentials. This is not to say, however, that you should not read them critically, or that they are guaranteed to be correct or work for your particular school or context.

1.5 What topics does this book cover?

Chapter 2 begins by exploring the definitions of formative assessment as well as the history of the term, and lays out a framework for the whole book. Next, **Chapter 3** examines the most fundamental question in the literature: *what is the relationship between assessment and feedback?* In particular, the chapter explores what evidence tells us about making feedback effective, and what this might mean for student learning. **Chapters 4 and 5** presents the evidence around cognitive science and assessment, making a case for the pre-eminence of this approach in understanding assessment, and the importance of metacognitive development. **Chapter 6** examines an element which rarely features prominently in discussion of formative assessment: *peer learning*, exploring the opportunities and challenges you will face when implementing peer learning effectively. Given the questions that the evidence raises for educators, **Chapter 7** examines what this means for designing effective assessments and curriculum structures for students. It examines the evidence for the effectiveness of different types of assessment design and curriculum structure. After exploring the evidence for the individual elements of formative assessment, **Chapters 8 and 9** focus on how formative assessment has been successfully implemented in schools and studies, examining the common errors of implementation that have been made, and reflecting on the evidence from a decade of attempts to make formative assessment work at a system-wide level. As part of this discussion you will be able to reflect on what it means to put this into practice in your classroom.

Chapter 2
Mapping the area

2.1 Chapter overview

This chapter will outline:

2.2   a brief history of formative assessment;

2.3   a research map on assessment;

2.4   what the strongest claims are that can be made from the evidence;

2.5   what the important questions are to ask about formative assessment.

2.2 A brief history of formative assessment

'Can assessment raise standards? Recent research has shown that the answer to this question is an unequivocal "yes".' This was the claim made at the start of *Beyond the Black Box*, the influential 1999 Assessment Reform Group report into formative assessment in the classroom (Broadfoot et al, 1999, p 1). When exploring the literature on assessment, it can be common to encounter this kind of claim, which in turn makes it easy to think that assessment is settled and uncontroversial. The reality is that while there is a consensus view that assessment can be used to improve learning, there are lots of different explanations as to *how*. In this chapter, we will explore the evidence about assessment, and lay out both the history of research in the field and the major claims which have been made.

It would be wrong to think of formative assessment as a recent innovation. The term was first used by Michael Scriven (1967) who made the distinction between formative and summative approaches to assessment. The first large-scale evidence of the impact of formative assessment was gathered in reviews by Natriello (1987) and Crooks (1988), with both authors concluding that using assessment to evaluate performance during learning can have a powerful impact. Since then, the most powerful advocates for the approach have been Black and Wiliam (1998a, 1998b; Wiliam, 2011). Their work showed how formative assessment could lead to substantial learning gains and they discussed potential effect sizes of between 0.4 and 0.7, which would be considered extremely large in the context of other educational interventions.

> **Question**
> **What is effect size?**

> **Answer**
> This is the headline figure that some types of meta-analysis produce, an attempt to statistically measure the difference between two groups. In education terms, it usually measures the impact of introducing the intervention on a group of students, against a similar group of students who have not received the intervention. This is a standard statistical measure in scientific research but its use in education has been controversial. Hattie (2008) famously used them to compare different educational techniques, but his critics have pointed out that they are in some ways inappropriate tools to measure effect as they decontextualise the interventions, and offer a relatively crude measure of efficacy (Snook et al, 2009; Terhart, 2011).

Black and Wiliam's work (1998a) was followed by a shorter practical review called 'Inside the Black Box' (Black and Wiliam, 1998b), which condensed the findings for a wider educational audience and initiated a discussion of the implications of their findings for education policy. In the UK at least, this can be seen as the point at which formative assessment began to be visible in national debates about education.

The term 'Assessment for Learning' (AfL) was popularised in the subsequent report by the Assessment Reform Group (1999). This report proposed that AfL should become a central focus of the government's drive to raise classroom standards. They argued that it should be given far greater prominence in initial teacher training, school management and inspection. It was at this point that formative assessment began to be talked about as an important way to improve UK school standards. The years since the report have been dominated by an odd combination of successful research in favour of formative assessment, and mixed success at implementing formative assessment in the classroom. Black and Wiliam translated their findings into the King's Medway Oxford Formative Assessment Project (KMOFAP; Black and Wiliam, 2005) to demonstrate the impact that these findings could have on real-life classrooms. This research found positive effects of formative assessment when properly applied to classrooms (Black and Wiliam, 2003; Black et al, 2003; Wiliam et al, 2004). Similar research found positive effects of formative assessment techniques in Latvian high school students (Olina and Sullivan, 2002), New Zealand science teaching (Bell and Cowie, 2001a, 2001b), American K-5 schools (McDougall et al, 2007), fifth grade students in US schools (Chen and Andrade, 2016), and middle school science students (Yin et al, 2014). The Organisation for Economic Co-operation and Development (OECD) examined formative assessment across a range of different school cultures and published a policy brief document which, despite identifying individual issues within certain countries, gave an overall very positive overview of the power of assessment (Organisation for Economic Co-operation and Development, 2005).

While this body of evidence was accumulating, in the UK at least there was a clear divide emerging between results in the research studies and results on the ground. In 2004, formative assessment was adopted by the National Strategies as a key policy for school improvement. However, Ofsted reviewed the impact of this programme and subsequently released a report in 2008 which found inconsistent implementation, with an impact on achievement which was *'no better than satisfactory in almost two thirds of schools visited'* (Ofsted, 2008, p 5). A similar detailed report into primary education appeared at the same time, which showed the same pattern of strong impact when properly applied, but inconsistency both across and within schools when techniques were poorly understood or implemented (Department for Education and Skills, 2007). Individual country studies also identified several systemic challenges in diverse education systems such as Sweden (Jonsson et al, 2015), Scotland (Hutchinson and Hayward, 2005) and Singapore (Lim and Tan, 1999), which suggested that implementation was far from straightforward. Recent major articles have been more cautious about the efficacy of formative assessment and have raised questions about the socio-cultural implications of assessment reform (Baird et al, 2014, 2017).

So where does this leave the study of formative assessment? Among the teaching profession, it is commonly believed that assessment can be an effective tool for improving learning, even though formative assessment is lacking an overwhelming evidence base. As a result, there has been a shift in focus away from testing the effects of formative assessment, and towards implementation of assessment reform and the individual cognitive processes which can affect assessment design. Wiliam's latest book (2016), for example, characterised formative assessment as a critical element of the wider process of school reform.

Why has assessment reform not always succeeded?

Why have the gains we have seen in classroom research experiments not been replicated across the entire system? There are two potential explanations for this available:

1. The claims may have been overstated or misinterpreted in some way.

2. The implementation of formative assessment in the classroom may be more complex and difficult than had originally been implied.

It is true that there has been some confusion regarding the strength of the original claims made by Black and Wiliam (1998a). Bennett (2011) argues that these reviews were given the status of meta-analyses, a much higher level of statistical robustness than a literature review. While reviews systematically compare the literature, they do not statistically measure overall effect, making overall claims of effectiveness more subjective. This probably led to a misunderstanding of the claims about effect sizes and the strength of evidence available at the time. However, as we will explore later in the chapter, this probably does not invalidate the overall claims of impact. On the second point, however, there can be little doubt that formative assessment is more difficult to implement than many had originally hoped. National initiatives to implement formative assessment have been accused of misinterpreting it, and of failing to separate it from summative accountability measures. Wiliam was quoted in the *TES* as saying:

> **There are very few schools where all the principles of AfL, as I understand them, are being implemented effectively... We have (DfE officials) saying: 'We tried AfL and it didn't work.' But that's because (they) didn't try the AfL that does work.**

(Stewart, 2015)

Evidence now suggests that if formative assessment is brought in as a bolt-on solution to regular teaching, particularly in high-stakes summative cultures, it has limited effect. For formative assessment to become effective it must be embedded within a self-improving educational community where space is made for effective CPD and professional reflection.

2.3 A research map on assessment

Emergence of the formative/summative distinction in assessment

Scriven (1967)
Bloom (1969)

Initial reviews of assessment research

Fuchs and Fuchs (1986)
Natriello (1987)
Crooks (1988)

The emergence of modern assessment and AfL

Black and Wiliam (1998a, 1998b)
Pellegrino et al (2001)
Stiggins (2005)
Wiliam (2011)

Debate, extension and challenge

Stiggins (2002)
Kingston and Nash (2005)
Dunn and Mulvernon (2009)
Bennett (2011)
Baird et al (2014, 2017)

Classroom research into assessment

Cowie and Bell (1999)
Buchanan (2000)
Thompson et al (2004)
Wiliam et al (2004)
Black and Wiliam (2005)
Winiger (2005)
Ruiz-Primo and Furtak (2006)
McDougall et al (2007)
Chen and Andrede (2016)

Studies into the implementation of formative assessment

OECD (2005)
Black et al (2003, 2004)
Ofsted (2008)
Hopfenback and Stobart (2015)
Hopfenback et al (2015)
Hayward (2015)
Tigelaar and Beijaard (2015)
Wiliam (2016, 2017)

Research into individual elements of assessment

FEEDBACK

Early studies and meta-analyses
Bangert-Drowns et al (1991)
Kluger and DeNisi (1996)
Black and Wiliam (1998a)
Narciss and Huth (2004)

Major modern reviews and meta-analyses
Hattie and Timperley (2007)
Shute (2008)
Wiliam (2011)

PEER LEARNING

Meta-analyses
Springer et al (1999)
Colliver (2000)
Prince (2004)
McMaster et al (2006)
Johnson et al (2006)
Strobel and van Barneveld (2009)

Cognitive approaches to peer learning
Kirschner et al (2006, 2009)

ASSESSMENT AND CURRICULUM DESIGN

Overviews
Pellegrino (2002)
Kelly (2004)
Wiliam (2011)
Christodoulou (2017)

Deliberate practice
Ericsson (2006, 2016)

Criticisms
Hambrick et al (2007)
Macnamara et al (2014)

COGNITION AND MEMORY

Overviews
Willingham (2010)
Brown et al (2014)
Didau and Rose (2016)

Cognitive load theory
Sweller (1994)
Kirschner (2002)
Pass et al (2003)
Kirschner et al (2009)
Plass et al (2010)

Retrieval practice
Karpicke and Roediger (2008)
Karpicke et al (2009)
Karpicke and Blunt (2011)
Roediger and Butler (2011)

Spaced learning
Karpicke and Bauernschmidt (2011)
Karpicke and Roediger (2007)
Smolen et al (2016)

METACOGNITION AND SELF-REGULATED LEARNING

Metacognition
Schraw et al (2006)
Veenman et al (2006)
Lai (2011)
Didau and Rose (2016)

Self-regulated learning
Butler and Wynne (1995)
Nicol and Macfarlane-Dick (2006)
Dignath et al (2008)

Formative assessment at different levels and scales

Formative assessment has always been subject to a plurality of definitions. For instance, there are two different models of formative assessment, as characterised by Wiliam (2016, p 125):

Table 2a Types of formative assessment

Improving student achievement with instructional data teams	Setting up assessments and reviewing results in teams to identify students who are under-performing, and responding with interventions.
Building teacher quality through classroom formative assessment	Training teachers to teach in a formative way, so that minute-to-minute in the classroom, children are exposed to ongoing formative assessment and feedback.

Of the two models, classroom formative assessment has evidence of greater impact, 16 instead of 30 points on the Programme for International Student Assesment (PISA) scores – regular comparative international assessments conducted by the Organisation for Economic Co-operation and Development (OECD) – over two to three years (Wiliam, 2016, p 125), but these are not mutually exclusive approaches and most schools who are implementing formative assessment programmes will look at implementing both models together.

There also differing timescales at which formative assessment can be conducted. This was characterised by Wiliam and Thompson (2008) and summarised by Wiliam (2016, p 114) into three cycles: short-cycle, medium-cycle and long-cycle.

1. **Short-cycle –** minute-by minute in lessons, and lesson-to-lesson;

2. **Medium-cycle –** from a week, up to a month;

3. **Long-cycle –** from monthly through to yearly.

These different timescales are important because formative assessment can be different depending upon the timescale used. At the shortest timescale, formative assessment is focused on the relationship between teacher and student, and the exchange of information on performance to adjust teaching and learning. As the timescales widen, it begins to offer information which can be used to explore wider issues of curriculum design and cohort-level impact. For example, in the classroom you might be able to learn what issues the students are having with a particular question, whereas over the course of a year it might reveal issues with the overall approach to a topic.

ous proxy for learning is, of course, performance in externally
s. Indeed, our education system is founded upon the notion that
is a reliable one. However, this means that in most systems data
is su. .ative, not formative. Formative assessment differs because it shifts focus away from summative assessment and places value on ongoing classroom assessment. A common misinterpretation of formative assessment is that it is something that is merely pre-summative, but this can rob assessment of its formative value. Wiliam and Thompson (2008, p 68) explain that:

> **assessment is formative for individuals when they can use the feedback from the assessment to improve their learning. Assessment is formative for teachers when the outcomes from the assessment, appropriately interpreted, help them improve their teaching, either on specific topics, or generally.**

The value of formative assessment is in how *both* teacher and student react to assessment, and what happens after assessment is in many ways more important than the assessment itself.

One significant challenge to this model is the fact that learning is itself an extremely tricky thing to identify and measure. As Soderstrom and Bjork (2015) show, there is a large body of evidence that learning is distinct from performance, and assessments themselves do not directly reveal learning. But as Wiliam (1998, p 3) notes, *'validity is therefore not a property of tests, nor even of test outcomes, but a property of the inferences made on the basis of these outcomes'.* Formative assessment does not directly capture learning, but is the process whereby teachers and students can make valid inferential judgements about the learning which has taken place. Given that it is actually impossible to truly capture what is taking place inside 'the black box' of the classroom and the students' minds, we must accept that assessment is a tool to aid professional judgement and not to replace it entirely. Equally though, given the considerable evidence of the impact of formative assessment strategies, we must accept that these strategies mean that *something* is happening inside the minds of students to move learning forward, even if we can never capture and measure it perfectly.

2.4 What are the strongest claims that can be made from the evidence?

The research has revealed five major elements of formative assessment which all have substantive bodies of evidence to support their claims of efficacy (Wiliam, 2011):

1. Clarifying and understanding learning intentions and criteria for success.

2. Engineering effective classroom discussions, questions and tasks that elicit evidence of learning.

3. Providing feedback that moves learners forward.

4. Activating students as instructional resources for each other.

5. Activating students as owners of their own learning.

The evidence for these claims will be explored in more detail in each of the subsequent chapters but they are drawn from a diverse range of studies. In some cases, the effectiveness of a particular aspect of assessment is clear, whereas in other cases it is not as clear whether it is the effect of the intervention itself, or other supporting factors. There is no coherent model of formative assessment used across studies, so different research may emphasise different elements to a greater or lesser extent. This picture may seem complex but, based on the best evidence available at present, we can reasonably claim that:

• these five elements are individually and collectively impactful on learning;

• these elements can be used by teachers to improve learning in their classroom;

• successfully implementing these elements effectively is dependent upon specific conditions of training and institutional culture.

Of course, even these more limited claims lead us somewhere potentially very powerful. Given that implementing formative assessment is something that can be implemented by teachers themselves, we have evidence of an approach that is readily available and which can meaningfully improve learning. If all this positivity is exciting, it must also be tinged with caution. There are some very important challenges which need to be addressed first.

2.5 What are the important questions to ask about formative assessment?

The most detailed and sustained critique has been by Bennett (2011, p 5), who identified five issues with formative assessment. It's important to note that this was constructive criticism, which he hoped, once raised, would prompt *'a frank and judicious dialogue, one that is necessary for moving this promising concept forward'*, not an attempt to discredit it entirely.

Table 2b Issues within formative assessment, adapted from Bennet (2000)

The definitional issue	What is formative assessment? Is it a definable thing, or are we grouping together separate things under a single banner?
The effectiveness issue	Is formative assessment as effective as has been claimed by proponents?
The domain dependency issue	Can we understand formative assessment as a set of techniques which go beyond domain (subject) knowledge? Or is the interweaving of domain knowledge and pedagogical knowledge so complex that it is difficult to conceive of formative assessment as a coherent intervention in its own right?
The measurement issue	If formative assessment is based upon measurement of students' learning, how confident can we be in the measurement itself? Are our assessments creating valid data, or does it not matter? Can formative assessment ever be anything more than professional inference?
The professional development issue	Given how powerful the effects are claimed to be, and how warmly they have been embraced, why has their impact been negligible at a system-wide level? How can we get teachers to use formative assessment successfully?

Are these issues fatal to formative assessment?

The most fundamental of the challenges to formative assessment is the possibility that it might not actually exist. It must hastily be added that by 'not exist' we don't mean that there is no evidence for it, but that there might be no secure, stable entity to which we can affix this evidence. There has been substantial evidence for the efficacy of many of the underlying components, but it is possible that in the rush for something substantial, we may be grouping together related (but distinct) phenomena into an artificial whole. The challenge this presents to implementing formative assessment is obvious and in his paper Bennett suggests that it might impact research as well:

the research covered is too disparate to be summarized meaningfully through meta-analysis. That research includes studies related to feedback, student goal orientation, self-perception, peer assessment, self-assessment, teacher choice of assessment task, teacher questioning behaviour, teacher use of tests, and mastery learning systems. That collection is simply too diverse to be sensibly combined and summarized by a single effect-size statistic.

(Bennett, 2009, p 5)

The original claims were made with reference to substantial effect sizes of 0.4–0.7, and when seized upon by educational reformers, these numbers took on a robustness that they had never been intended to have. As Black and Wiliam (1998b) have made clear, this was never meant to be taken as evidence of a formal meta-analysis process. Wiliam has publicly stated that the way in which this number was dealt with '*may have been a mistake*' (2016, p 115) but he is also keen to point out that they were reasonably consistent with other studies at the time, and despite a subsequent weakening in the claimed effect (down to 0.34) this still represents a powerful impact upon learning that we would be foolish to dismiss. He argues that while it is okay to have critical discussions about the magnitude of the effect, the breadth of evidence makes it impossible to dismiss the powerful effects of the phenomenon entirely.

The professional development issue

The failure of attempts to implement formative assessment at a national scale has had the effect of both toning down the claims, and honing the assumptions about implementation into more specific models. But rather than leading us to conclusions of 'emperor's new clothes', the cause of the problem may be more mundane. The truth is, formative assessment was widely misunderstood and poorly implemented. The issue seems to have been one of fitting it into existing school cultures. Given the diverse nature of formative assessment, particularly the two different models (data review teams vs in-class formative assessment), schools have been biased towards the former model. This is because it is the version of formative assessment which most neatly fits into the high-stakes testing culture, as many institutions already had a framework of assessments for accountability purposes. This has, in many cases, been implemented as pseudo-summative testing with very little impact or effect. In many schools, despite an increase in assessment, '*teachers rarely pitched work precisely enough to students' understanding and prior learning*' (Ofsted, 2008, p 9). When poorly understood like this, formative assessment is reduced to mere assessment. The good news is that when properly understood and culturally embraced by an institution, the evidence shows that formative assessment can have a transformative effect, particularly as it '*acts as something of a Trojan horse into wider issues of pedagogy, psychology and curriculum'* (Wiliam, 2009, p 13). As we will see in Chapter 7, solving the professional development issue for formative assessment might mean addressing professional development issues in the profession as a whole.

2.6 Summary

Formative assessment is the name given to a reflective mode of practice which uses assessment to improve the learning process. The features most strongly identified as part of formative assessment are clarifying learning aims, on-going classroom assessment and feedback, metacognition and peer learning. There is substantial evidence that the components of formative assessment have a powerful impact upon learning. However, the evidence does not offer a comprehensive and clear model which can be adopted straight off the shelf and be placed in the classroom with a guaranteed effect. The focus is now on the relationship between assessment and learning environment. It is entirely possible that formative assessment has become a component in a larger model of evidence-based pedagogy which encompasses other cognitive, professional and behavioural research.

Formative assessment remains one of the most effective interventions in terms of cost and impact that has yet presented itself, but we need to exercise caution in how we engage with the evidence, otherwise it is likely that we can make interventions which then fail to deliver. Too often, formative assessment can be reduced to summative practice testing or assessment as accountability, and this can often be to the detriment of more effective forms of formative assessment. The evidence suggests, however, that through careful teacher training for teachers of all ages and experiences, and an appropriate learning culture, even greater effectiveness may be achieved.

Questions for enquiry in your own school

- Is your assessment primarily formative or summative?

- To what extent do you use elements of formative assessment already?

- What effects could you secure through better use of assessment?

Exploring further

Embedded Formative Assessment is the best all-round overview, but Wiliam's chapter on formative assessment in *Leadership for Teacher Learning* (2016) is also excellent for summarising the recent debates and issues. Many of his articles and useful blog posts can also be found on his website: www.dylanwiliam.org/

- Wiliam, D (2011) *Embedded Formative Assessment*. Bloomington, IN: Solution Tree Press.

- Wiliam, D (2016) *Leadership for Teacher Learning: Creating a Culture Where All Teachers Improve So That All Students Succeed*. West Palm Beach, FL: Learning Sciences International.

ResearchEd have an excellent summary of the debate around formative assessment available on their website, written by Mary Whitehouse of the York Science Education Group. www.workingoutwhatworks.com/~/media/researched/red%20files/briefings/formative-assessment.pdf

For some of the debates and controversies, the best summary of the issues is Bennett, R E (2011) Formative Assessment: A Critical Review. *Assessment in Education: Principles, Policy & Practice*, 18: 5–25, or Baird, J, Hopfenbeck, T, Newton, P, Stobart, G and Steen-Utheim, A (2014) *State of the Field Review: Assessment and Learning*. Oslo: Norwegian Knowledge Centre for Education.

Chapter 3
Assessment and feedback

3.1 Chapter overview

This chapter will outline:

3.2   key ideas about assessment and feedback;

3.3   what the evidence says about assessment and feedback.

3.2 Key ideas

Most models of how assessment can improve learning involve the use of feedback. However, feedback, like formative assessment, is a concept which is generally endorsed, yet is also often misunderstood. Pretty much everyone intuitively understands that assessment always produces some sort of feedback, even if just through the grade students receive at the end to let them know if they passed. However, meta-analyses into feedback (Bangert-Drowns et al, 1991; Kluger and DeNisi, 1996; Black and Wiliam, 1998b; Narciss and Huth, 2004; Hattie and Timperley, 2007; Shute, 2008) have revealed a range of complex interactive effects and counterintuitive findings that make putting the evidence into practice far more complex than the simple claim that feedback is good. All teachers give feedback in some form or other, but what allows it to make the leap to being 'formative'? To answer this question, this chapter will explore the long history of feedback research and explore the complex (and still evolving) evidence-based model of feedback that has emerged. One thing will rapidly become clear: feedback isn't simple.

What is feedback?

Feedback is a term borrowed from engineering systems, where it means returning output from a system back to the original input, and using this process to adjust performance. A home thermostat is a good example of a system that uses feedback. Simplistic early models of classroom feedback tended to follow this model closely. In these models, the student gives an output in the form of assessment, and this is then fed back to the student to improve their performance, either by motivating them to work harder or allowing them to think about what they need to do next. This model of feedback, however, is not formative. As has been established in the previous chapter, the value of formative forms of assessment is that assessment is used to alter and refine future learning. In formative models of learning, feedback is not raw data, but carefully chosen and relevant output data which causes learners to reflect and improve. Data that is not chosen specifically to improve learning or which does not carry this purpose is not formative, and is potentially distracting noise for students and teachers. Hattie and Timperley (2007, p 397) are therefore careful to stress the formative aspect when they describe feedback as *'information provided by an agent (e.g., teacher, peer, book, parent, self, experience) regarding aspects of one's performance or understanding'* whose purpose is *'to reduce discrepancies between current understandings and performance and a goal'*. A powerful principle of feedback in learning, as opposed to feedback in engineering systems, is that feedback from the student to the teacher is as critical as the feedback from the teacher to the student. Unless a teacher examines and reflects upon the results of assessment, then feedback cannot have any impact on any future guidance they provide.

As the research definition of feedback has become more formative, it has also motivated researchers to reconsider how feedback is used in the classroom. Shute (2008, pp 166–67) argues that besides closing the gap between performance and goal, feedback also acts as a cognitive scaffold during the learning process, which in turn allows learners to develop deeper understanding about learning itself. Hattie and Timperley (2007) similarly stress that the best forms of feedback do more than offer feedback on the task itself, and actually start to reveal the whole learning process to the student.

The variables of feedback

Feedback studies are enormously varied, and to understand the scope of the research evidence, it is useful to map the various variables of feedback that have been identified:

Table 3a Variables of feedback, adapted from Hattie and Timperley (2007), Shute (2008) and Wiliam (2011)

Specificity	The level of information present in feedback messages.
Feedback complexity/ length	Related to specificity, this is how the information is presented in terms of length and complexity of information
Timing	How immediately the feedback is generated and how immediately the student can act upon the feedback.

Response certitude	How certain the students are in the correctness of their own answer.
Learner level	How the age or ability of learners affects the efficacy of the feedback they should receive.
Group or individual	Whether the learner receives feedback on individual performance or as part of a group.
Goal orientation	How the motivation and focus on a final goal affect the kinds of feedback given.
Normative feedback	The extent to which the feedback provides a comparison with the student's peers and the impact that this has.
Direction	Whether the feedback is *from* or *to* the student.
Directness	The extent to which the feedback is a direct correction or an invitation to think about how to correct themselves.
Agency	The person who generates the feedback. Is it a teacher, the student themselves or a peer?
Form	Whether the feedback takes the form of a grade, a comment, a task or something else.

As the range of these variables makes clear, there is no simple way to conceptualise feedback; making effective research into feedback is hard. Researchers can either choose a model of feedback that is too broad to pinpoint effective components, or else they look at a single variable in detail and in doing so miss interaction effects between the variables. This is why the succession of literature reviews into feedback have been so useful. By comparing effects across a range of studies they have begun to reveal the patterns that can only be perceived at a broader level.

The primary impact of these large comparative analyses has been to give a narrower definition of feedback that captures the difference between regular and formative forms.

- **Feedback** – linear, from student to teacher, consists of raw output of the student's performance and value, presented without a framework for how to use it.

- **Formative feedback** – multidirectional, generated by teachers, students and peers, carefully chosen, leads to tasks and opportunities to think and improve.

The most thought-provoking discovery has been the variables of *direction* and *agency*. Feedback was generally conceived of as a linear transmission from the assessment to the student (via the teacher), but increasingly this model is inadequate. The right kinds of assessments can lead to peers and students themselves generating relevant feedback. In fact, you may need to rethink it as *'a process whereby students actively construct their own knowledge and skills'* (Nicol and Macfarlane Dick, 2006, p 199) with an ultimate focus on the skill of self-regulating their own learning. Feedback shouldn't just focus on making you better at a task or skill, but at learning itself. Similarly, understanding that feedback is a two-way process is transformative to how we use it. What teachers learn from students via assessment can have more impact upon the learning journey than individual feedback to a student. Without good assessment, teachers cannot make the changes to practice that are necessary to improve learning.

3.3 What does the evidence say?

How robust is the evidence?

The first thing that needs to be addressed are the issues with the research into feedback. Kluger and DeNisi (1996) reviewed the research on feedback and found that only 131 of the 3000 studies they reviewed met reasonable standards for effectiveness and validity. While the quality of studies has largely improved since then, much of the research still has one or more of the following problems:

1. It uses very small sample sizes and yet makes broad claims.

2. It uses research methodologies which fall significantly short of those of a large-scale randomised control trial (RCT).

3. It focuses on adult learning environments (frequently second-language learners), making it difficult to infer its efficacy in other educational environments.

4. It focuses on short-term effects of feedback, not long-term effects.

Despite a succession of reviews over several decades (Bangert-Drowns et al, 1991; Kluger and DeNisi, 1996; Black and Wiliam, 1998b; Narciss and Huth, 2004; Hattie and Timperley, 2007; Shute, 2008), no singular model of feedback has emerged. Instead, these reviews have revealed the powerful interaction effects of different variables of feedback. More recent reviews have drawn a line under the idea of a single universal model of feedback and have instead begun to establish broad models of efficacy that highlight basic principles which hold true in in most circumstances, but which may not easily be replicated without careful thought.

Effective forms of feedback

It would be logical to argue that feedback is inherently a good thing, given its prominent role at the heart of most models of learning, but the evidence is much less clear than you might think. In Kluger and DeNisi's review (1996) they found that 50 of the 131 robust studies they reviewed actually showed a negative impact of feedback upon performance. This is starkly counterintuitive to many of our professional assumptions about feedback, and this points towards the care required when trying to reduce research to universal teaching principles. Hattie and Timperley's review (2007) showed that effective feedback can only be explored in the context of the different levels which it operates at. They argue that there are four different levels of feedback, not all of which are effective.

Table 3b The four levels of feedback, adapted from Hattie and Timperley (2007, pp 90–96)

Type of feedback	Abbrevi-ation	Content	Effectiveness
Feedback about the self as a person	**FS**	Evaluations of the learner as an individual.	Not effective in developing learning.
Feedback about the task	**FT**	How well tasks are understood or performed.	Effective in developing learning, but limited.
Feedback about the processing of the task	**FP**	How well understood is the main process needed to understand and perform tasks.	An effective form of feedback.
Feedback about self-regulation	**FR**	Feedback to self that monitors, directs and regulates actions.	An effective form of feedback.

Feedback on the self alone is counterproductive to performance, as it tends to distract students and affect motivation. Task feedback does have evidence of a positive effect, but their major finding was that its power was significantly less than that of process feedback and self-regulation feedback. These two forms of feedback focus on developing the learner, not just their performance on a task, and this ultimately leads to more permanent learning gains. This points to a challenge in how we think about feedback. If we only ever focus on short-term task improvements in performance, we may make it harder to improve long-term learning, but if we want to see progress, we tend to focus on short-term measures of success. Of course, teachers also sometimes focus exclusively on task feedback due to pressures of accountability and exam focus. Christodoulou (2017) argues that a major barrier to the implementation of effective formative assessment in UK classrooms has been the reduction of assessment to an exam focus. Assessment structures can force teachers to give task feedback to the exclusion of feedback that stimulates deeper forms of learning. In order to combat this and create deep and meaningful learning through feedback, you need to take account of the following key findings from the research:

Feedback must be correctly focused

To create feedback that is effective, we need to integrate all the dimensions of feedback together. For example, Hattie and Timperley (2007, p 87) say that an effective model of feedback answers three questions:

- *Where am I going?*

- *How am I going?* (ie how am I performing?)

- *Where to next?*

However, crucially, they also say that the best feedback answers all three questions *at once*. The problem with a lot of feedback is that it may answer one or two of these in isolation. For example, when students complete an assessment and are given a grade, they are often also told how close they are to a target grade. This might tell them how they are doing, and even give them a sense of where they are headed, but it fails to tell them how to get there. It is therefore quite easy to design feedback that is ineffective, and it is quite a challenge to design feedback that also allows students to grow a wider awareness of the learning process.

Feedback should cause appropriate thought and action

Wiliam states that *'If I had to reduce all of the academic research on feedback into one simple overarching idea... it would be this: feedback should cause thinking'* (Wiliam, 2011, p 127). This is probably the bottom line for producing effective feedback. Information that doesn't cause thought or reflection is just comment, not feedback. One term that has been used to describe this idea is *feedforward*, which was borrowed from psychological studies of feedback in business (Kluger and Nir, 2006). This term captures the idea that feedback should inherently lead to thought and action.

Table 3c Thinking and non-thinking approaches

Type of feedback	Thinking (feedforward)	Non-thinking
Written comment	A question about the work that requires a response from the student.	Offering an evaluative comment on the student's effort.
Highlighting errors	Highlighting errors and asking the student to correct them.	Putting corrections on the text and returning it.

Of course, the danger with this approach is that teachers can very easily take something that ostensibly causes thought (for example, writing a comment) and do it in such a way as to make the thought unproductive (eg commenting on something irrelevant). In addition, *when* the feedback is received can also affect how it is received. There is growing evidence that delaying feedback can improve its efficacy (Mullaney et al, 2014; Mullet et al, 2014), but only if the students are interested in the response, and the same studies have also found that students tend to prefer to receive feedback immediately. So far, the evidence is inconclusive, and we should not perhaps be seeking to delay all feedback in the classroom. Indeed, there is some evidence that immediate feedback is better than delayed feedback on some tasks (Opitz et al, 2011).

The other problem for teachers is that knowing how to stimulate thought is essential to creating effective feedback. Students need to be thinking about the right things and in the right way, and what this looks like may vary significantly depending upon the level of mastery the learner already has. Students with low levels of mastery may only be able to cope with clearer, simpler feedback, whereas students with high levels of mastery may be able to cope with more sophisticated forms of feedback and take more responsibility for correction themselves. To turn feedback into understanding, students need a level of awareness of both the skill itself and the learning process. A failure to process feedback effectively can lead to over-confidence, or flawed corrections that can deepen errors and worsen performance (Bjork et al, 2013). Of course, students need our guidance and feedback to progress from low to high levels of mastery. This is why it is important that teachers are aware of the role of metacognition in the learning process, and why feedback should begin to grow this awareness in students. This topic will be tackled in detail in Chapters 4 and 5, where the role of memory and metacognition will be looked at carefully, but for now it is worth also considering the ways in which the student's perception can affect their response to feedback.

The psychological state of the student affects the efficacy of feedback
Both of the previous rules that have been outlined should be understood to have an asterisk beside them, marking them as *under the right circumstances*. The truth is, there are powerful interactive effects from other variables of feedback that mean it is difficult to say that a single model of effective feedback exists. As Hattie and Timperley (2007, p 100) explain, '*feedback is not only differentially given but also differentially received*'. Feedback must not only match content, but also context. Key factors that affect student response to feedback include:

- **Response certitude** – the extent to which students felt their answer was right in the first place. Kulhavy and Stock (1989) showed that the greater a student's certainty that their answer was correct, the more time was spent on correction when they found out that they were wrong. In general, the more confident a student is that their answer is correct, the more likely that error is to be corrected by feedback. This is called the *hypercorrection effect* and it has been replicated in a variety of studies since (Butler et al, 2011; Metcalfe and Finn, 2012; Van Loon et al, 2015).

- **Methods of assessment** – students also want to know how they compare to their peers (a particular problem in curve-grading systems). Again, this seems to interact negatively with feedback effects. Students are not only more focused on achievement than feedback, they are more focused on what other students are getting than they are on their own feedback (Butler, 1988). If you want students to focus on mastery of the academic domain, then they need to be assessed against criteria for progress, not each other (Butler, 2006).

- **Contextualising and anticipating feedback** – unless teachers provide context to understand the feedback they are receiving, students often interpret formative assessment as summative assessment, affecting their motivation for further study (Pollard and Triggs, 2001). Similarly, if students are encouraged to anticipate feedback, it positively affects their engagement (Pekrun et al, 2014).

These examples show that the teacher should choose feedback strategies which are psychologically appropriate for the individual or group they are working with. Simplicity and consistency are both useful for creating more stable psychological states among students.

Rethinking feedback

The many complex interactions and problems with the research can cause us to want to abandon feedback entirely, but this would be an unwise conclusion. Instead, it is more helpful to say that feedback demands professional experience and subject knowledge. Designing feedback that addresses all the possible variables at once may well be impossible in the reality of the classroom. Feedback doesn't have to be perfect to have a positive impact. For example, while individualised feedback may be potentially superior, the time cost may be prohibitive. Well-designed group feedback could be better for a teacher if it allows them to better manage the students' attention, give them more structured practice time overall, or saves time for more instruction. Broadly combining the evidence with good classroom habits and strong professional knowledge is likely to produce feedback strategies which work. As long as it is broadly meeting the criteria for good feedback, teachers should not punish themselves about whether it is completely optimal. As Shute (2008, p 162) concludes, *'providing feedback that is specific and clear... is a reasonable, general guideline'*. Similarly, the KMOFAP (King's Medway Oxfordshire Formative Assessment Project) study suggests that feedback should move *'away from systems, with its emphasis on the formative-summative interface, and re-locate it on classroom processes'* (Black and Wiliam, 2005, p 236). Effective feedback is indivisible from classroom context, and even wider social culture – to the extent that even whether your national culture is individualist or collective can affect your preference for different modes of feedback (De Luque and Sommer, 2000).

Finally, feedback is just one mechanism by which students progress; it is *'not the answer; rather, but it is one powerful answer'* (Hattie and Timperley, 2007, p 102). It is important to remember that there is a spectrum of teacher input from feedback to instruction, and many learning activities will span these two modes. If the instruction and assessment is good enough in the first place, the role that feedback will play is likely to be reduced.

3.4 Summary

Making feedback effective isn't easy, but there are potentially huge rewards on offer if you can work out how to make it work in your own particular context. The evidence doesn't offer an off-the-shelf model for effective feedback that you can easily implement. It does, however, suggest certain principles that may be effective when you are trying to build a better model of feedback in your own teaching:

1. Better feedback is focused, formative and promotes thinking.

2. The focus should be on the learning process itself, not just the specific task being undertaken.

3. Feedback can lose effectiveness if the motivations and goals of the learner are not taken into account, or the format chosen is not appropriate for the cultural or pedagogical context.

As a teacher, giving feedback requires us to think very carefully about how feedback is received and used by the student. It is not accurate to try to reduce feedback to strategies or interventions as this has the potential to eliminate the effective element in the feedback you give. Instead, we must look at selecting appropriate thinking tasks that respond to the findings of assessment, and which go beyond teaching students about the task itself, and reveal to them something about wider skills and the learning process.

Questions for enquiry in your own school

- How well are the principles of feedback understood in your school?

- Are the forms of feedback you practise in your school used to promote thinking and reflection?

- Do you make effective use of peer- and self-feedback strategies?

- To what extent do you think about context when you give feedback to students?

Exploring further

The best place to start if you want to know more about feedback is to read the major reviews:

- Kluger, A N and DeNisi, A (1996) The Effects of Feedback Interventions on Performance: A Historical Review, a Meta-analysis, and a Preliminary Feedback Intervention Theory. *Psychological Bulletin*, 119: 254–84.

- Hattie, J and Timperley, H (2007) The Power of Feedback. *Review of Educational Research*, 77: 81–112.

Chapter 4
Assessment and memory

4.1 Chapter overview

This chapter will outline:

4.2 key ideas about assessment and memory;

4.3 what the evidence says about assessment and memory.

4.2 Key ideas

Thus far, this book has focused on the formative element of assessment, the use of assessment to infer learning and the use of that knowledge to improve learning. This chapter doesn't deal with the evidence on assessment itself. Instead, it looks at other evidence from cognitive science that has implications for assessment, particularly those in relation to memory and cognition. Much recent research has looked more broadly at the phenomenon of assessment and concluded that the act of assessment is critical to the learning process. Assessment provokes recall and recall is fundamental to the learning process, at least from the perspective of our long-term memory. Didau and Rose even argue that *'testing should not be used primarily to assess the efficacy of your teaching and students' learning; it should be used as a powerful tool in your pedagogical armoury to help them learn'* (Didau and Rose, 2016, p 102) This chapter explores evidence that suggests we can leverage gains in memory through assessment, and thus produce better learning, and what implication that has for how we use assessment in the classroom. As some have argued (Pellegrino et al, 2001; Pellegrino, 2002), the findings of cognitive psychology have significantly challenged traditional assessment practice and that reform requires a combined approach that addresses all three legs of the *'assessment triangle'.*

Figure 4a The Assessment Triangle, adapted from Pellegrino (2002, p 49)

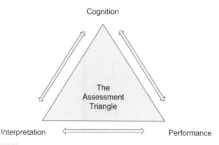

As Pellegrino explains *'advances in the sciences of thinking and learning need to be used for framing the model of cognition, which must then inform our choices about what observations are sensible to make'* (2002, p 50). While developments in psychometrics and improvements in the use of statistics mean that we have better tools for understanding interpretation and performance than ever before, without an understanding of the cognition of learning, we may be measuring something without value to learning. To understand how good assessment works, we must first examine the evidence on how learning works.

Memory and assessment

One of the most famous models in educational theory is Bloom's taxonomy (Bloom, 1956), a hierarchy of modes of thinking that places knowledge and understanding as lower forms of thinking, while creative and evaluative forms and thinking are higher. The impact of this model has been to encourage teachers to avoid focusing on lower forms of thinking and instead focus on creative and evaluative thinking. Psychologists have questioned the validity of Bloom's taxonomy as an accurate model of the cognition of learning (Bereiter and Scardamalia, 1998), with one critic claiming *'the hierarchical structure of the cognitive domain of the Taxonomy is in violent disagreement with the plain evidence of the nature of the learning process'* (Moore, 1982, p 29).

Thinking of knowledge as a 'lower' skill can have a profound effect on assessment and learning as the focus of assessment tasks becomes exclusively on 'higher' forms of thinking. Acquiring knowledge is therefore seen as a secondary benefit of the pursuit of these higher forms of thinking, rather than a critical prerequisite. Many traditional teaching practices are based upon this fallacy. Schemes of work, for example, were originally predicated on the notion that covering the material was equivalent to learning it. The task of securing the knowledge in memory was seen as a task for the student during later revision (even the word *revision* itself is derived from a French-Latinate root, meaning 'to see again'). The problem with this approach is that there is no evidence that exposure is an effective way of establishing memory. Indeed, it may even be harmful as it can lead to what Brown et al (2014, p 15) call *'the illusion of knowing'* where students can feel as if they have learned, despite no actual improvement in long-term memory. Brown et al (2014, p 3) show that there is a second model, which has been called *retrieval practice*:

- **Exposure** – through repeated exposure to the material that is being learnt, the student builds up memory of the material;
- **Retrieval practice** – the student is engaged with the material and then is repeatedly required to retrieve the material from memory.

Repeated studies have shown that retrieval practice is the only meaningful method by which knowledge can become effectively secured in long-term memory (Karpicke and Roediger, 2008; Karpicke et al, 2009; Karpicke and Blunt, 2011; Roediger and Butler, 2011). Assessment is a tool by which retrieval practice can take place. Students who are directed to repeatedly access and make use of relevant memory can strengthen that memory for future use, making it more accessible and eventually something that the student 'just knows'. Of course, one main challenge for teachers is managing the learning so that what is actually being committed to memory is of value. Poorly managed retrieval practice is worse than no retrieval practice at all. If a student creates a flashcard in which they confuse the definitions of *mitosis* and *meiosis*, every time they use that flash-card they are deepening their error and making their knowledge less accurate.

Question

This sounds like rote learning, and isn't rote learning ineffective?

Answer

There are two ways to answer this question. Firstly, it's possible to misunderstand what 'rote learning' means. Rote simply means to repeat. Its association with an industrial model of education is unfair. Secondly, rote really describes what psychologists call *retrieval practice*, and as you shall see in this chapter, retrieval practice works best when varied and extended, so even if a student does start with repeated retrieval practice, this should be developed later.

Schemas

It is worth mentioning a useful concept from psychology here, that of a *schema*. The term schema refers to the organised structures of knowledge we construct in long-term memory when we learn. An example of schemas in learning is when children learn times tables. While it is possible to learn the multiplication process as a standalone process in working memory, we tend to use long-term memory to make low-level multiplication possible. Children repeatedly use retrieval practice to establish schemas of multiplication tables in their long-term memory, which they can draw upon when necessary without having to individually calculate sums in their heads. This frees up mental resources to focus on how these can be used in other, more complex, sums.

In educational terms, the creation of effective schemas is a large part of any cognitive model of learning. Schemas give structure to knowledge and therefore ease of access and control. It's the difference between looking up something in a room full of randomly stacked books compared to looking it up in a neatly stacked library. A student who knows their times tables will be able to draw on that knowledge with minimal effort when applying knowledge about multiplication, and therefore not be wasting working memory. This matters because there is a clear cognitive relationship between knowledge and thought. In particular, knowledge acts as the building blocks of thought:

> **Knowledge does much more than just help students hone their thinking skills: It actually makes learning easier. Knowledge is not only cumulative, it grows exponentially. Those with a rich base of factual knowledge find it easier to learn more—the rich get richer. In addition, factual knowledge enhances cognitive processes like problem solving and reasoning. The richer the knowledge base, the more smoothly and effectively these cognitive processes—the very ones that teachers target—operate.**

(Willingham, 2006, p 30)

This directly contradicts the hierarchical nature of Bloom's taxonomy. Assessment that focuses on knowledge is not assessment wasted on 'lower' skills. It can have a direct and cumulative effect upon the acquisition of higher-order skills such as analysis and comprehension. For example, many 'higher-order' skills can be improved through focusing on improving knowledge. Take, for example, essay writing, an ongoing challenge for most teachers. While writing an essay may seem to be a primarily skills-based domain, those skills are all supported by clear teachable schemas of knowledge:

- relevant vocabulary;
- knowledge of essay structure;
- useful phrases;
- subject knowledge.

It is possible to teach and assess all of these skills, providing a better foundation from which the higher skills can emerge. Knowledge and skills are indivisible, and choices made in assessment need to reflect this.

Cognitive load theory

Exploring cognitive science also introduces one of the most significant issues in assessment and curriculum design, *cognitive load theory* (CLT). Many modern attempts to rethink assessment have made use of CLT (Sweller, 1994; Paas et al,

2003; Plass et al, 2010). CLT explores the implications for learning when the two human memory systems are properly understood.

Table 4a Types of memory

Working memory	This is the memory used in conscious experience. It processes the world as you experience it. Working memory is limited, and can typically only hold a small number of items in it.
Long-term memory	This is where we store our knowledge for use when we need it. Long-term memory is vast and can be drawn upon at minimal cognitive cost.

In order to learn, students must first hold knowledge in working memory, but to have actually *learned* that knowledge it needs to pass into long-term memory through practice and retrieval. Working memory is the gatekeeper to long-term memory, so it is imperative that teachers manage the load they place on working memory. To judge cost effectively, teachers need to be aware of the difference between *intrinsic load, germane load* and *extraneous load*, outlined in Table 4b.

Table 4b Types of cognitive load

Type of load	Definition
Intrinsic load	The inherent cognitive load required to complete a task, ie the basic thinking cost.
Germane load	Some additional load beyond the minimal intrinsic load is to be welcomed as it is the cost of organising and systematising memory. Germane load refers to cognitive effort that has a positive effect, defined as *'the mental resources devoted to acquiring and automating schemata in long-term memory'* (Debue and van de Leemput, 2014, p 1101). While there is some debate about whether germane load is actually distinct from intrinsic load, the concept shows us that minimising load does not mean that learning should be easy.
Extraneous load	Cognitive load which is not relevant to the specified learning.

Assessment design therefore must find the appropriate blend of intrinsic and germane load, while avoiding placing any extraneous load on cognitive operations.

Finding the correct balance of cognitive load is a real challenge for teachers. If we build an assessment that is too complex, students will not have the schemas in long-term memory to succeed and will thus fail and learn nothing. However, if we build a task that is too easy (ie too heavily scaffolded or not challenging enough), students will not be required to build new schemas for future use and therefore will succeed, but not actually learn. Of course, if the task is challenging, but in the wrong way, then it will be challenging but not produce learning. For example, if students are asked to draw pictures with a story they are writing, they might focus attention on this task, leaving little working memory free for writing. The issue of cognitive load is tackled in further detail in Chapter 7: 'Assessment and Curriculum Design' (pp 64–71).

4.3 What does the evidence say?

The evidence shows that the structure of memory should affect how we plan and use assessment. By understanding how leveraging memory can improve learning, we can derive principles for good assessment design.

Assessment as a driver of learning

The power of assessment goes beyond making formative reflection possible. Taking part in assessment also helps students' learning because:

- It encourages students to take part in 'retrieval practice', the accessing of information from memory, which strengthens the memory for future use.

- When appropriately directed, it helps students build organised schemas of knowledge in long-term memory, which help them to think more effectively and reduce the cognitive load of tasks.

- It offers repeated opportunities to practise learning, and learning is something that takes place *across* lessons, not within a single iteration.

- Didau and Rose (2016, p 102) claim that this knowledge-building function of assessment is actually more important than its role in formative assessment:

Rather than pretending that the assessments typically used by teachers can give us valid, fair, useful, and reliable sources of information which can track student progress in learning, we might be better off seeing its purpose as building students' storage of the knowledge and skills we wish them to remember and apply. Beyond drawing useful formative inferences about student learning from assessment, we can advantage our students by making use of the testing effect.

If correct, this would mean that we are looking at assessment from the wrong angle. Formative assessment is a secondary prize to developing memory and knowledge. However, the evidence directly comparing these two effects is limited, and the issue also becomes irrelevant when you realise that they are not necessarily in competition, nor mutually exclusive. If both are effective, we want to use both.

What does the evidence say are the best ways to use assessment to leverage memory? Brown et al (2014) summarise four key principles neatly in their excellent book *Make it Stick*:

Table 4c Principles of leveraging memory to improve learning, adapted from Brown et al (2014, pp 23–160)

To learn, retrieve	Retrieval practice is the basis for establishing memory.
Mix up your practice	Interleaving activities and making use of the power of forgetting can reinforce memory and learning.
Embrace difficulties	Learning must be effortful to be effective. Easier isn't better.
Avoid illusions of knowing	Use assessment and other tools to calibrate your judgement of your learning.

To learn, retrieve

There is strong evidence that using assessment as retrieval practice has a strong positive impact upon learning because it strengthens pathways and allows students to reconstruct learning in their heads (Karpicke and Blunt, 2011, p 772):

> **Not only does retrieval produce learning, but a retrieval event may actually represent a more powerful learning activity than an encoding event. This research suggests a conceptualization of mind and learning that is different from one in which encoding places knowledge in memory and retrieval simply accesses that stored knowledge. Because each act of retrieval changes memory, the act of reconstructing knowledge must be considered essential to the process of learning.**

Over the years of retrieval practice research, there have been lots of individual findings about the best ways to apply retrieval practice. Retrieval practice can be effective even without feedback, but feedback enhances the benefits of testing (Roediger and Butler, 2011), so an effective approach will likely use both. Delaying feedback can also improve its efficacy (Pashler et al, 2007). Repeatedly studying content gives no improvement to performance, but testing does (Karpicke and Roediger, 2008) so repeating content should be replaced by retrieval testing, such as low-stakes quizzing. Retrieval practice is also significantly more effective than elaborative study strategies such as concept-mapping, suggesting that retrieval is more powerful than asking students to self-construct their own schemas of knowledge (Karpicke and Blunt, 2011).

Mix up your practice

In a school system focused on summative outcomes, there is often a culture which encourages pedagogy which can be described as *massed practice* – doing the desired task repeatedly in order to make progress with learning. The evidence suggests the complete opposite may be true. Varying both the conditions of practice and the thing being practised leads to more durable learning. This effect has been found in retrieval of words (Cepeda et al, 2006), motor skills (Lee and Genovese, 1988) and pictures (Hintzman and Rogers, 1973). Longer retention requires longer intervals between practices. If you want your memory to last longer from practice to test, you need a larger gap between practices (Pashler et al, 2007; Cepeda et al, 2009). This reveals another powerful cognitive effect that can be leveraged to improve retention, *spaced learning* (Karpicke and Bauern-schmidt, 2011; Smolen et al, 2016). This term simply means that by varying and spacing when the learning takes place, we make it easier for students to remember the information in the long term. The obvious implication of all this research is that rather than repeatedly practising the final exam, we should carefully structure assessment around the idea of varied, spaced practice.

Embrace difficulties

As a teacher, it is easy to regard your student's failure as the enemy. If the assessment used during lessons is the same as the task they will be assessed on at the end, then failure supposedly augurs failure in the future. However, one of the more striking findings to emerge from the research is the fact that failure and forgetting, when properly marshalled, can have a positive impact upon learning. Take memory, for instance:

> **Psychologists have uncovered a curious inverse relationship between the ease of retrieval practice and the power of that practice to entrench learning: the easier a knowledge or skill is for you to retrieve, the less your retrieval practice will benefit your retention of it. Conversely, the more effort you have to expend to retrieve knowledge or skill, the more practice of retrieval will entrench it.**

(Brown et al, 2014, p 79)

Remembering something in a moment is very little evidence that a long-term schema has been built. Memory requires *consolidation*, a process whereby it must stabilise and settle through retrieval and usage (Dudai, 2004). This can easily be disrupted by the limits of working memory, as well as other cognitive distractions. Massed retrieval practice can hold it in working memory for a sustained period, but the creation of long-term schema requires it to be partially forgotten, then effortfully retrieved. Difficulty enhances the significance of the memory, and therefore its future recall.

Similarly, Bjork (1994) had coined the term *desirable difficulty* to describe the idea that a managed and relevant level of difficulty is really important for effective learning. Difficulties exist that enhance learning by forcing deep cognitive engagement, leading the brain to build more secure and better schemas to deal with those tasks in the future (Bjork and Bjork, 2011). Forms of difficulty like failure on assessment, or forgetting crucial information, are powerful learning tools, provided they offer opportunities to think in the relevant way. Even some confusion itself can lead to improved performance on tests, although only when it forces deep thought about the thing that is actually required to be studied (D'Mello et al, 2014).

Much assessment conflates learning with performance on tests, and we tend to infer that learning has taken place because of apparent gains in performance. But if you assess students using tasks that are too easy, or which are so heavily scaffolded that students can complete them easily without thinking hard or deeply, then you will not be able to infer anything meaningful about their long-term learning gains. Similarly, small gains from massed practice might be mistaken for fundamental learning. Introducing carefully managed difficulty, reinforced with retrieval and spaced assessment, is likely the optimal model for acquiring deep learning.

Avoid illusions of knowing

Taken as a whole, the discipline of psychology has largely revealed how weak and prone to bias human cognition is. Within education, this manifests as a tendency to see learning taking place when in fact there is little direct evidence of it. This is the product of a cluster of cognitive biases around wanting our students to do well, or believing effort indicates learning. For example, students often choose to just read through notes rather than undertake more cognitively difficult, but effective, strategies, such as quizzing to test their memory. Rereading notes feels like learning – you pass the information through your head and gain a sense of renewed familiarity – but without practising accessing and using the schemas of knowledge, there is no improvement in their strength or effectiveness.

These *illusions of knowing* are extremely dangerous. They waste time and can give students a false representation of their ability, which can lead to problems with motivation, or the extent to which they listen to feedback. Assessment must be carefully constructed to circumvent these limitations as best they can. Switching from reading notes, to rewriting them from memory, for example, turns this activity into something of cognitive value. Assessment offers a tantalising glimpse of learning, but it never securely captures what is happening, so there are several principles we need to follow to design assessment which avoids the traps of illusions of knowing:

- When judiciously used, formative assessment offers a way to circumvent biased personal observation, but when conducted badly, it can reinforce those biases. It is worth exploring ways to remove bias from assessment such as blind marking of papers, or methods which do not rely on subjective application of marking criteria, such as *comparative judgement* (Pollitt, 2012).

- Formative assessment should test the things that are of value to summative assessment, but these may not be the same as the summative assessment itself. We need to break assessment down into the constituent knowledge required to execute a skill, and test each element in a meaningful and quantifiable way (Christodoulou, 2017).

4.4 Summary

Cognitive science has completely revolutionised how we look at assessment. The most notable finding is that assessment is a necessity for good learning, and its power to reinforce memory may play an even greater role in the progression of learners than the mechanism of formative assessment. Good assessment practice should make use of the key findings of cognitive science. In practice, this means that assessment:

- uses the assessment effect to build effective schemas of knowledge in long-term memory, so as to not overwhelm working memory;

- encourages retrieval practice;

- is spaced appropriately to encourage deep retrieval;

- plans desirable difficulties into the assessments and is not afraid of effortful learning;

- is aware of the dangers of falsely thinking that assessment results show learning.

- Does your school have a culture of retrieval practice embedded into lessons?
- To what extent do you plan lessons to take account of the cognitive load on your pupils?
- To what extent does your assessment structure assess individual components of the subject being learnt? Or do you assess the whole thing in the form of past papers?

The most easy and obvious first steps towards cognitively smart assessment is to build retrieval practice into your everyday lesson design. Simple steps include:

- using multiple-choice quizzes to recap information;
- using recap questions after sections of the lesson with direct instruction;
- using starter quizzes at the beginning of lessons to recap information from previous lessons;
- building retrieval practice into larger schemes of work, allowing time for forgetting between quizzes.

Exploring further

There are several excellent books available on memory, cognitive psychology and learning.

Daniel Willingham's (2010) classic *Why Don't Students Like School?* is an excellent overview of the relationship between memory, knowledge and learning.

- Willingham, D T (2010) *Why Don't Students Like School? A Cognitive Scientist Answers Questions about How the Mind Works and What it Means for the Classroom.* 1st ed. San Francisco, CA: Jossey Bass.

Make It Stick (Brown et al, 2014) takes a practical walk through the research evidence, while discussing the implications for curriculum design.

- Brown, P C, Roediger, H L and Mcdaniel, M A (2014) *Make It Stick: The Science of Successful Learning.* Cambridge, MA: Harvard University Press.

What Every Teacher Needs to Know About Psychology is a hugely sensible, robustly evidenced and referenced guide to the psychological research available. It focuses the classroom teacher and offers neat summaries at the end of each chapter.

- Didau, D and Rose, N (2016) *What Every Teacher Needs to Know About Psychology.* Melton, Woodbridge: John Catt Educational Ltd.

The Learning Scientists (www.learningscientists.org/) are a group of American psychologists and cognitive scientists who provide free resources on effective learning for use with colleagues and students.

Chapter 5
Metacognition and assessment

5.1 Chapter overview

This chapter will outline:

5.2 key ideas about metacognition and assessment;

5.3 what the evidence says about metacognition and assessment.

5.2 Key ideas

Like formative assessment, metacognition is one of the evidence-based learning approaches whose popularity is ubiquitous, but whose definition can seem fuzzy. It is probably best conceived as a multidimensional set of skills that involve *'thinking about thinking'* (Lai, 2011, p 33). In education, this is also linked to the idea of teaching awareness of the learning process. In the literature, metacognitive ideas can often be found under the sister term *self-regulated learning*, which implies taking overall ownership of the learning process. This chapter will explore the most useful definitions of metacognition and the evidence on how to develop it in the classroom.

Broadly speaking, the evidence of the importance of metacognition is strong. The Education Endowment Foundation Toolkit summarises metacognition as having '*high impact for very low cost*' (Education Endowment Foundation, 2017b) and gives +8 months' advancement as the likely impact on learning. Hattie's famous comparative study of evidence-based interventions gives an effect size of 0.53 for metacognitive strategies (Killian, 2017). The evidence strongly suggests that metacognition is integral to the learning process, and strategies which specifically seek to improve it have proved effective in a range of different contexts. This chapter will look at the different processes which have been identified as metacognitive, and explore the evidence on how these can be improved in the classroom.

Metacognition

In its stricter, narrow definition, metacognition has two constituent parts (Lai, 2011):

Table 5a Components of metacognition

Knowledge about cognition	Knowing how you learn and what impacts your cognition. Knowledge of how cognition works during learning. Knowledge of effective cognitive strategies and when to use them.
Monitoring cognition (cognitive regulation)	Relating your cognitive progress relative to goals. Comprehending and being aware of learning as it takes place. Selecting appropriate strategies and using them effectively.

Metacognition is the growing awareness of the learning process that takes place as a student begins to understand their mind and develop processes to make learning increasingly effective and efficient. Experienced learners can learn more efficiently and effectively than inexperienced learners because they can make better use of their cognitive resources. Metacognitive learning also piggy-backs onto the regular learning process. Cognitive knowledge is gained through cognitive regulation and vice versa. The issue for teachers and for those planning assessments around metacognition is exactly how best to manage this relationship to maximise overall learning.

Question
When do children start to learn metacognition?

Answer
There is a lot of debate over the exact nature of when metacognitive skills begin, often predicated on what definition of those skills you are using. Very young children struggle with actual metacognition, and the age often given for formal metacognitive acquisition is around eight to ten years. Children often need to develop underpinning cognitive skills like *theory of mind* (a knowledge that others have thoughts and perspectives) first. The process is likely to resist simple age gradations though, as it is difficult to separate it from environment, education and the individual. As Veenman et al (2006, p 8) explain, *'metacognitive knowledge and skills already develop during preschool or early-school years at a very basic level, but become more sophisticated and academically oriented whenever formal education requires the explicit utilization of a metacognitive repertoire'*.

Broader definitions of metacognition

In practice, discussions of metacognition in teaching regularly wander into territory that is not strictly part of the core metacognitive model, such as motivation, mindset and critical thinking. To discuss these issues critically, it is important to understand that these individual terms are fluid and often very locally defined. Some researchers, such as Schraw et al (2006), have argued that we need to bring these skills together under the wider banner of *self-regulated learning*, suggesting that metacognition is just one component alongside a larger battery of cognitive processes and motivation. These debates are interesting but probably don't help the classroom teacher understand metacognition. Instead, it is important to explore the key concepts that make sense of metacognition.

Domain-specific skill versus general skill

Evidence on the existence and usage of these wider skills is frequently embedded in a wider debate about the extent to which each of them can be meaningfully defined as separate from other cognitive processes or knowledge. There is significant debate about the extent to which these skills are *domain-specific* or *general*:

Table 5b Domain-specific and general skills

Domain-specific	Skills which are domain-specific are functionally indivisible from related domains of knowledge, so if a skill is domain-specific it can't be transferred to other domains and is dependent upon the knowledge base within that domain.
General	General skills are independent of local domains and can be used across different cognitive areas. They work regardless of local knowledge.

The critical thinking that is undertaken by an engineer is likely to be domain-specific, and not readily transferable to another domain, such as art. This debate is relevant to understanding metacognition because if metacognition is indeed domain-specific, it would require it to be taught differently in different academic domains.

Executive function and metacognition

It is hard to discuss metacognition and cognition without mentioning the umbrella concept of executive function. While metacognition generally describes the regulatory processes associated with cognition and learning, psychologists consider them part of a larger cognitive process called executive function. This is the set of functions related to organising, directing and monitoring mental processes. This relationship is important because educational metacognition (learning how to learn) is a relatively narrow cognitive process compared to wider acquisitional processes such as learning self-discipline or how to follow cultural norms. The Center on the Developing Child at Harvard University (2017) note that *'children aren't born with these skills—they are born with the potential to develop them'*. This is, by extension, true for metacognition as well. When we consider metacognitive acquisition, we need to be aware that it is built upon a platform of other cognitive skills, and understand its place in wider cognitive development. This has implications for early years teachers, as a lack of control over executive function is an impediment to learning skills like reading (Cartwright, 2012).

Assessing metacognition is difficult

Metacognition is difficult to measure through assessment because '*metacognition is not always explicitly heard or seen during task performance*' (Veenman et al, 2006, p 6). This has perhaps led in the past to it being overlooked as a vital element of any model of assessment. Gains made through massed practice can mask the lack of metacognitive learning taking place, and an absolute focus on summative assessment can lead teachers to not put any value in teaching metacognition. However, a more holistic model of the learning process must recognise the importance of metacognitive learning if the eventual destination of learning is to be independent, self-regulating learners. Assessment has a critical role in the iterative process of using and regulating cognitive knowledge, as it provides a measure of performance and can be used to direct student reflections on learning.

5.3 What does the evidence say?

Is metacognition domain-specific?

This is the most fundamental question that may impact upon how metacognitive skills are taught and assessed. Some studies have been conducted into the topic and have generally found a combination of both general and domain-specific elements. Studies by Scott and Berman (2013) and Fitzgerald et al (2017) have found that that the skills of metacognitive knowledge and regulation are general, but the ability to do them accurately is domain-specific. Similarly, Neuenhaus et al (2011, p 163) found that despite evidence of domain-specificity, there is '*a strong relation between general metacognitive knowledge and domain-specific metacognitive knowledge*'. At the moment, the strongest claim we can make is that there is a complex relationship between general metacognitive skill and domain-specificity. It is likely that domain-specific knowledge is necessary to make metacognitive learning effective, but that there are some common elements between metacognitive skills in different domains. From the perspective of a teacher devising assessments, it is plausible that we might be able to apply common approaches, but using our domain-specific knowledge as subject experts to refine these approaches to work in our subject area.

Teaching metacognitive skills

If the goal of teaching metacognition is to activate students as agents of their own learning, then two logical conclusions we might draw are that we should get students to do as much of the work on their own as we can, and that we should directly teach metacognitive skills alongside other aspects of learning. However, the issue of general versus domain-specific elements clouds both of these assumptions.

Let us look at the issue of peer assessment. Students who lack domain-specific knowledge cannot effectively assess the efficacy of their own learning and therefore cannot build effective metacognitive knowledge. As teachers, we bring a huge amount of domain-specific knowledge and experience to the marking process. Students can never truly replicate that and there is even a danger they may draw the wrong conclusions from reviewing a paper themselves. But this doesn't mean that we should therefore reject these techniques entirely. However, it does impose limitations on the freedom we give students, and the ways we use assessment to make students reflect upon their own learning.

The second assumption that could be made is that there is some sort of shortcut to metacognitive skill that can be accessed through programmes that teach metacognition as a general cognitive skill. A review by Jacob and Parkinson (2015) found no good evidence that improvements in executive function are teachable as independent skills. This is not to say that metacognition itself is not teachable, but that we must look to the domain-specific level to have any impact. As metacognition is interwoven into the learning process itself, then the acquisition of metacognitive knowledge is not distinct from learning a domain and cannot be taught as such. This means that we need to explore strategies that make the metacognitive knowledge visible to students as they are learning. Assessment is the critical tool by which we do this, as it provides the best opportunity for students to apply cognitive knowledge to provide cognitive regulation – to evaluate and reflect on their work, they must acquire and apply knowledge about learning itself (Butler and Winne, 1995).

Designing assessment to develop metacognition

The first thing that is necessary to accept when planning assessment is that it is pretty much impossible to measure metacognition in the classroom. While under the controlled conditions of psychological experiments, trained researchers can find ways to isolate and measure aspects of metacognition; that option is simply not available to classroom teachers. Metacognition is internal, poorly defined and difficult to separate from cognition itself. This should not be a problem for classroom teachers, however, as our focus is on the measurable proxies for learning such as performance on tests. If we see improvements in outcomes following metacognitive interventions, we can remain happily agnostic about measuring the exact process.

The relationship between assessment and metacognition is twofold. Firstly, in terms of metacognitive knowledge, certain forms of assessment provide knowledge of the underpinning structures. This reflects the distinction made in Chapter 3, the difference between task feedback and process/metacognitive feedback. Well-chosen assessment can direct a learner to think about not just the essay they are currently writing, but *all* essays they write. Feedback can help reveal the same things, and provide feedforward opportunities to practise the wider skill. The second way that assessment is linked with metacognitive learning is in teaching metacognitive regulation. Students need to gain experience of applying appropriate cognitive strategies to fine-tune their application of cognitive knowledge.

Scaffolding assessments to grow metacognition

A scaffold is any tool or resource that a teacher uses to make a task more understandable. In terms of cognitive load theory, a scaffold is a tool designed to lessen the cognitive load for the student, and therefore make more complex tasks accessible. Examples of common scaffolds include: partially worked answers, providing an essay plan, multiple-choice questions.

The metaphor of the scaffold has been criticised by some researchers as it can be taken to imply that the scaffolding makes progress possible in such a way that it becomes dependent upon the scaffolding itself. Indeed Lepper et al (1997) suggest a better metaphor may be something like a tunnel support, as once progress has been made and the support has been removed, the structure remains as robust as before. This difference is indeed critical if we want to understand the best ways of using scaffolding in assessment design. Research into cognitive load has shown how mastery is only acquired through extensive guided practice from experts. Students are unable to practise effective self-regulation of learning until quite late in the progress and '*the advantage of guidance begins to recede only when learners have sufficiently high prior knowledge to provide "internal" guidance*' (Kirschner et al, 2006, p 75).

The principles a teacher follows can be summarised as follows.

- Metacognitive scaffolding looks very different at different ages and levels of mastery. At the youngest ages of education, it may not be effectively metacognitive at all, and instead focuses on executive function, or basic regulative cognitive functions.

- At ages where metacognitive scaffolding is possible (8+ years), teachers should choose techniques which are appropriate for the level of mastery the student has arrived at. In practice, this means heavy scaffolding early in the process that is kept in place until quite late in the learning journey.

- Early in the process, scaffolds may focus on establishing knowledge in memory or allowing students to begin to deliberate practice with concepts that are too difficult to understand by themselves. However, as component units are steadily mastered there needs to be a shift towards removing scaffolding, or using scaffolding which directs attention towards awareness of connections and fundamental structures.

Puntambekar and Hubscher (2005) argue that models of learning that are more open to peer and collaborative forms of learning will require more complex notions of scaffolding. They reject the notion that scaffolding should primarily refer to a model of direct instruction. This is an interesting position, but more research needs to be done to properly understand what this could look like. One interesting intervention model is that of Mannion and Mercer (2016), a battery of collaborative and metacognitive learning tasks under the title Learning to Learn (L2L).

Choosing scaffolding techniques is highly dependent upon the nature of the task, but the following factors should be taken into account when designing appropriate scaffolding for complex tasks:

Table 5c Factors for determining scaffolding in complex tasks, adapted from Reiser (2004, pp 284–95)

Focus effort	Make students spend cognitive effort wisely and monitor their own progress towards goals.
Elicit articulation	Make students be explicit about their reasoning and thinking.
Elicit decisions	Make students make decisions that require them to make use of their knowledge.

Surface gaps and disagreements	Make tensions in concepts and solutions visible and make students accountable for solving them.

Clarity

Clarity in task-setting, sharing learning objectives and assessment criteria has been one of the most widely adopted aspects of formative assessment practice. These practices build metacognitive awareness through clarifying how and what the students should be thinking about. This is good educational practice by itself, as it raises the efficiency of learning by not wasting students' attention (White and Frederiksen, 1998), but it also has metacognitive value if teachers explain not just *how* but *why*. Students who better understand the purpose of the task or the shape of the learning are better able to discern the underlying structures of learning and knowledge and therefore bootstrap their own learning more effectively (Wiliam, 2011).

However, this has not been without issues, as this has often been reduced to 'putting the objectives on the board' or other oversimplifications. Wiliam (2011, pp 51–69) argues that clarity in setting objectives only works if the target is achievable and meaningful. Vague, irrelevant or improperly focused learning objectives will lead to failure. To achieve appropriate focus, he suggests the following criteria:

- Decide what learning you wish to deliver.

- In some cases, decide the learning objectives in partnership with the students (while giving due respect to the academic authority of the teacher).

- Separate learning from context and task to produce learning which can be transferred to different contexts.

Provide self-monitoring structures

For assessment to lead to an awareness of learning itself, it is necessary to use metacognitive regulation to build metacognitive knowledge. Through the act of selecting strategies, applying them and reflecting on their success, learners can begin to build robust knowledge of the efficacy of certain strategies, and the general ways in which learning and knowledge work. To that end, a critical element of assessment that builds metacognition is providing structures which allow the student to self-monitor their own progress and reflect on *how* they are learning, not merely *what*. Examples of techniques like these include:

- regular assessment that leads to reflective exercises;

- comparing their own answers to model answers;

- rewriting answers using worked examples;

- regular personal reviews of assessment.

Using assessment to build memory and reveal comprehension

Another critical element in building metacognitive awareness is the use of assessment to build memory and show both the teacher and student what has been comprehended. Low-stakes assessment can be used to build *Metamemory*. Metamemory is a critical metacognitive skill that means growing an awareness of how your memories are stored and how your own memory works. It can speed processing of memories and allows students to pick better strategies with their memory in the future. Assessment that builds Metamemory uses the following principles:

- Assessment should make memory visible to the students and give them an opportunity to reflect on and react to failures in recall.

- Assessment should be planned from the beginning around a stable core of knowledge. This is not to say that recall is not challenged or extended, but that what is being recalled is clear to the teacher and student throughout.

- Resources for retrieval practice should be clear and consistent, and be used in such a way to provide easy feedback and correction. The range of resources should be restricted to an effective core to discourage the cognitive costs of switching and allow the students repeated practice with the same structures. This should lead to better, clearer schemas in the students' long-term memories.

- Once efficient recall has been established, students should be taken through assessments which scaffold the process of using the knowledge in context, growing progressively more complex as they begin to achieve mastery.

One innovation that has emerged in recent years is *knowledge organisers* (Kirby, 2016, p 58), minimal visual maps of critical information that are used as a teaching tool for learning knowledge. The exact form these take is subject-dependent, but typically these might consist of key terms, diagrams, vocabulary and other relevant information. The rationale for their use is as follows:

- They force teachers to reflect on what is meaningful information, and therefore focus teaching on an effective core of knowledge.

- The students are given a clear sense of what they are expected to know and do not spend their cognitive resources on trying to discern what is important and what is not. Similarly, they can better digest what they are required to know as it is clearly presented.

- If concepts are effectively visualised, this can bring into effect 'dual coding' (Mayer and Anderson, 1991; Kuo and Chiang, 2015), the dual use of auditory and visual memory systems, as a way of reinforcing memory.

- The availability of a focused core of knowledge makes planning, assessing and developing resources for teaching easier.

Similarly, Christodoulou (2017) argues that high-quality textbooks are excellent for delineating and structuring knowledge in an optimal way.

Feedback

Feedback is a good example of how subject knowledge makes better learning possible. One of the assumptions made by many models of feedback is that there is a lot of individual variance in student performance. Feedback is assumed to help students work out how they personally vary from a model of ideal performance. The reality is that while students do vary widely in the extent to which they deviate from a model of ideal performance, they do not vary much in *how* they deviate. It is usually a matter of degrees of error, rather than each student inventing a unique way to fail. *What are my students getting wrong as a group?* is probably a more useful question for a teacher to ask than *what is each individual student getting wrong individually?* As Hattie and Timperley (2007, p 99) noted in their review of feedback research, there is a continuum of instruction and feedback. What we call feedback is often just a second, more calibrated attempt to give instruction and opportunities to practise. In many cases, the best way to tackle issues in learning is not to offer detailed feedback on individual mistakes, but to look at common errors, adjust the instruction accordingly and give students a chance to practise them again. Feedback should not focus on how to do better on the test, but on teaching students the structures and processes that underpin the assessment, and it should also help them to understand the whole learning process (what Hattie called *process feedback* and *feedback about self-regulation*). Only teachers with good subject knowledge can execute this effectively.

5.4 Summary

Metacognition is an awareness of the processes which underpin cognition and of cognition itself. In educational terms, it refers to growing awareness of how we think and learn. Good assessment should not just be cognitively efficient, but should also develop metacognition as well. This way, the student grows as a learner overall, not just in the specific subject they are studying. Over time, this leads to better learning and more effective cognitive tools with which to tackle learning. When planning assessment, we need to deliberately think about metacognition, and using a cognitive model of learning is an important first step. If we use assessment to repeatedly give opportunities to students to see and experience how learning is taking place, they will become not just better at the subject, but the broader academic domain.

Questions for enquiry in your own school

- Do you plan lessons in such a way to make students aware of *how* they are learning, not merely *what*? Are you planning:

- How to evaluate their learning?

- How to monitor their learning?

- How to plan their learning?

- Do students use those strategies under guidance at first, before giving them an opportunity to use them by themselves?

- How structured is your approach to thought and memory? Is it structured in such a way to be easily mapped and comprehended by the student?

Exploring further

The relevant chapters in *What Every Teacher Needs to Know About Psychology* will give you a good overview of the key concepts and their relevance to assessment. Similarly, Lai's review of literature for Pearson, titled *Metacognition: A Literature Review*, is available for free online at http://images.pearsonassessments.com/images/tmrs/metacognition_literature_review_final.pdf.

- Didau, D and Rose, N (2016) *What Every Teacher Needs to Know About Psychology*. Melton, Woodbridge: John Catt Educational Ltd.

- Lai, E R (2011) *Metacognition: A Literature Review*. Always Learning: Pearson research report.

Chapter 6
Assessment and peer learning

6.1 Chapter overview

This chapter will outline:

6.2   key ideas about assessment and peer learning;

6.3   evidence for and against peer learning.

6.2 Key ideas

Peer learning has been a source of considerable debate in education over the past couple of decades. As will soon become clear, there is controversy about what peer learning looks like and what the evidence says about its efficacy. Some traditionalist models of education try to do away with it almost completely (Dyer, 2016), while some advocated methods see it as the ultimate prize of education, as they believe it has the unique capacity to prepare students for the challenges of the twenty-first century (Bell, 2010). It is described as one of the central pillars of formative assessment by Dylan Wiliam (2011) and is an important tool by which learners develop their learning skills. This chapter will explore the many different forms of peer learning, and present the best available evidence on how to make it work for you.

Varieties of peer learning

There are many different versions of peer learning available to researchers, and '*the terminology associated with group-learning approaches has become so entangled that it is difficult to distinguish between them, and there are unclear and even muddled messages in the literature*' (Davidson and Major, 2014, p 8). Often terms are used to group all these approaches to learning, such as 'student-centred learning' and 'active learning', often with subtly different emphasis. This book uses 'peer learning' as it is the closest thing to a neutral term available. However, broadly speaking there are six different types of peer learning:

Table 6a Forms of peer learning

Form of peer learning	Definition
Peer tutoring	One-to-one or small group tutoring by a knowledgeable peer.
Peer mentoring	Similar to peer tutoring, but the peer doesn't teach content, focusing instead on motivation, learning strategies and other metacognitive support.
Cooperative learning	Where students cooperate at a group level to achieve a learning task.
Collaborative learning	Distinct from cooperative learning in that students work not only in groups, but also with the teacher as well. In collaborative learning, there is also a focus on the individual within the group being accountable for their own learning.
Problem-based learning	Similar to cooperative learning, but this is a specific methodology of group learning organised around problem-solving tasks that teachers facilitate, but do not direct. The problem itself forms the locus for the group decisions and learning.
Peer feedback	Tasks that encourage students to generate feedback for their peers, either as a standalone task, or as part of teacher/self-feedback.

Assessment issues in peer learning

When choosing group work, the major challenge for assessment is deciding what teachers assess, and how they assess it. The sudden increase in complexity demanded by group work makes summative assessment particularly difficult as it suddenly presents the challenge of measuring learning effectively within the context of a group activity. Some forms of peer learning have group outcomes, (eg problem-based learning) while others use peer learning to support individual outcomes (eg peer tutoring). With peer learning, there will always be a tension between assessment at the level of the group and assessment at the level of the individual that adds an extra layer of complexity to how assessment can be used. Is success in a group activity a suitable method for inferring individual learning? Does feedback go to individuals or to the group? This complexity is one of the major challenges of picking group work over other forms of assessment. The question is whether this complexity is offset by potential other gains through a group-work approach (ie social skills/higher-order thinking skills) that still make it a superior strategy overall.

Factors that impact peer-learning assessment design

The great challenge of group-based learning is the complexities that it brings to assessment design. These emerge out of the complexities that were outlined in the previous section, but go beyond this issue alone. Topping (2005, pp 634–35) suggests a sizeable list of organisational variables, and the cost of these should always be accounted for when choosing peer-learning assessment design.

Table 6b Organisational variables that impact peer-learning assessment design (adapted from Topping, 2005)

Factor	Definition
Curriculum content	The knowledge/skills being learnt.
Contact constellation	The structure of the group, including the size of the group in relation to numbers of helpers/teachers.
Within or between institutions/classes	Whether learning is between classmates, or wider structures (some electronic forms of learning can create completely international groups).
Year of study	The age and stage of education the students are at.
Ability	Level of mastery the task draws on.
Role continuity	Whether members of the groups have consistent roles throughout.
Time	When the group work takes place, and for how long.
Place	The physical (or non-physical) space the collaboration takes place in.

Helper characteristics	The relative capability of people taking part – the interaction between high-skill and low-skill group members can severely impact group effectiveness.
Characteristics of the helped	For whom the peer learning is designed to help.
Objectives	What the desired outcomes of improvement are.
Voluntary	Whether the peer learning is self-selected, or assigned.
Reinforcement	The extent to which the group learning is reinforced by some sort of reward/motivation/check.

6.3 Evidence for and against peer learning

Is peer learning more effective than other forms of instruction?

This is the most controversial issue in relation to group work, as so many of the claims of peer-learning pedagogies rest upon it. The evidence is mixed on this issue and it is fair to say that while there is lots of evidence of the general efficacy of peer learning, its outright superiority to other forms of instruction is less clear. Similarly, what causes peer learning to be more effective is not easily explained from the existing evidence. Various reviews and meta-analyses have shown the efficacy of peer assessment. In higher education, Johnson et al (2006) found an effect size of 0.54 when comparing cooperation and competition, and 0.51 when comparing competition and individualistic learning. Similarly, a meta-analysis by Springer et al (1999) found an effect size of 0.51 for the impact of collaborative learning upon academic achievement. These are impressive effects and have led to very public shows of confidence in the superiority of peer-learning approaches. For example, Johnson et al (2014, p 10) claim that *'The research on cooperative learning is like a diamond. The more light you focus on it, the brighter and more multi-faceted it becomes.'*

However, as well as suggesting the power of peer learning, the evidence also reveals its complexity. Some peer-learning strategies have been found to be successful under certain circumstances, but not effective in others (McMaster et al, 2006). Prince (2004) describes the evidence as *'broad but uneven'*. Johnson et al (2000, p 14) found that *'the current research findings present a promise that if cooperative learning is implemented effectively, the likelihood of positive results is quite high. Results, however, are not guaranteed.'* The issues with the peer-learning evidence are summarised below.

- Many of the meta-analyses focus on studies from higher education and virtual learning environments, making it difficult to infer efficacy in other educational environments.

- Many of these studies compare peer learning with 'traditional methods' but the definition of traditional varies significantly, often just meaning 'what we normally do'.

- There is an overall lack of clarity about what exactly is being tested. Definitions and pedagogies vary from study to study. Links are frequently made between outcomes and mechanisms without a causal link having been clearly established.

- Some studies conflate learning improvements with secondary benefits of group work (confidence/independence/enthusiasm etc) in order to make claims of overall efficacy.

- As Kirschner et al (2009) show, many of the studies incorrectly infer individual learning from collective achievement.

Overall, the broad efficacy of peer learning has been established, but specific claims about peer approaches are more complex. More research is needed, particularly into whether the mechanisms for learning in different social learning techniques are comparable, and these should be followed by large-scale RCTs which compare specific techniques with specific modes of traditional instruction.

Cooperative and collaborative learning

The evidence from meta-analyses tends to suggest that collaborative forms of learning (group work including both students *and* teachers) have the edge over cooperative learning (entirely student-led) in the task of knowledge creation. Van Boxtel et al (2000) found structured collaborative tasks were more effective for concept learning than a more open group task. A study of project-based cooperative learning techniques found no improvement in outcomes (Menzies et al, 2016). Similarly, a review of meta-analyses in higher education concluded that *'the combination of teacher-centered and student-centered instructional elements is more effective than either form of instruction alone'* (Schneider and Preckel, 2017, p 591). The role of the teacher in designing and managing the group work is important and without it learning and group effectiveness can rapidly be lost (Mayer, 2002). In particular, teachers must build an element of individual accountability in assessment to maximise engagement and commitment (Morgan, 1994; Williams et al, 2005; Laal et al, 2013). Importantly, there are practical limitations to group learning that is not structured by a teacher. As Kirschner et al (2009) explain, *'it has become clear that simply placing learners in a group and assigning them a task does not guarantee they will work together'.*

This is not to say, however, that there is no good reason to choose unmediated group learning. If your focus is secondary skills such as confidence, student attitude or critical thinking, there may be value in a cooperative assessment design (Johnson et al, 2006). You must remember, however, that this may come at a time cost, and that structure remains critical. For example, Hmelo et al (2000) found promising evidence of cooperative learning leading to improved outcomes, but this was dependent on using highly structured assessment designs.

Peer feedback and peer mentoring

The evidence here is much clearer than for other forms of peer learning. There is a robust body of evidence that learning from a fellow student can work effectively (Rohrbeck et al, 2003; Ginsburg-Block et al, 2006; Liu and Carless, 2006; Nelson and Schunn, 2009b; Lloyd et al, 2015), although some of it comes from research into online virtual learning environments. The Education Endowment Foundation (2017c) rates the effectiveness of peer tutoring as '*moderate impact for very low cost, based upon extensive evidence*'. The strength of these two approaches seems to be based upon the fact that these can be conducted in a focused, structured way, and that both approaches are complementary to other teacher-led forms of instruction. Peer feedback is an excellent source of metacognitive learning, and peer mentoring is particularly effective as a supplement to regular classroom learning.

Problem-based learning

The evidence for the superiority of Problem-Based Learning (PBL) is particularly limited. Colliver's (2000, p 259) review found '*no convincing evidence that PBL improves knowledge base*', although other reviews have challenged this. Strobel and van Barneveld (2009, p 44) did a review of meta-analyses and concluded that '*PBL is significantly more effective than traditional instruction*'. A claim that PBL could lead to better knowledge retention seems particularly problematic and it is worth noting that five out of the eight meta-analyses reviewed in their study were of studies of PBL in medical training. The one meta-analysis in the review that focused specifically on knowledge acquisition found no positive effect of PBL, although they did conclude that '*students in PBL gained slightly less knowledge, but remember more of the acquired knowledge*' (Dochy et al, 2003, p 533). Capon and Kuhn (2004) did test PBL instruction against traditional lecturing and found that PBL was inferior to traditional lecturing for short-term memory retention, but that this difference disappeared later, and PBL learning allowed superior explanation of learning at a later date.

Given the limited evidence in support of the claim that PBL is a superior method for learning knowledge, many of the studies which support PBL instead argue for its superiority in skill acquisition and its ability to create more rounded, effective learners. As Loyens et al (2011) make clear, there is a need for more controlled experiments to form a more robust body of evidence. Certainly, there is no effective evidence base to suggest that problem-based learning should be adopted across the education spectrum

The cognitive argument

Cognitive science offers an argument why enquiry learning (such as certain types of cooperative learning and PBL) is likely to be ineffective. Kirschner et al (2006) argue that problem-based and student-centred learning fail to take into account the realities of human cognition. In particular, the limits of working memory capacity mean that without highly targeted scaffolding most students are likely to experience cognitive overload when presented with a difficult task and asked to solve it by themselves. Truly independent learning, it is argued, is not a reality for most learners and learning environments, and is restricted either to those who already have a high degree of mastery of the domain, or have extremely large working memory capacity. They do also stress the importance of balancing dependence and independence, so that the correct balance can be found between support and effort. Students whose work is too heavily scaffolded will require hardly any working memory and will not lay down good long-term memories for the future. It is worth noting that proponents of PBL have questioned the validity of this finding. Hmelo-Silver et al (2007) make the observation that these forms of learning are not 'minimally guided' and actually involve just as much careful scaffolding and feedback as more direct forms of instruction.

In a later paper, Kirschner et al (2009) go on to argue that cognitive load theory does not prevent effective collaboration; it's that most attempts at peer learning do not meet these criteria. They argue that peer learning could be especially effective for very difficult (and thus cognitively costly) tasks. In these circumstances, provided the group was set up correctly, participants might be able to combine their working memory capacities to tackle more difficult forms of learning. For example, if an individual is tasked with completing a crossword, and shares the clues with their friends, they may be able to complete more difficult crosswords than they could do by themselves. Sharing working memory and long-term memory make more challenging group tasks accessible. In contrast, low-difficulty tasks are usually less effectively tackled by peer learning because the additional cognitive load of managing group dynamics and resources outweighs any gains and reduces individual resources for task completion.

Evidence-based principles of effective peer learning

Although the evidence on this subject is diverse and of varied quality, we can still infer some good principles for peer learning in the classroom:

Peer-learning activities require a level of mastery

Group work is particularly unsuited for novices and younger learners as they have not yet acquired the schemas of knowledge required to succeed. Many proponents of self-directed modes of learning think that the evidence is so strong that it should be recommended as a universal pedagogy. The review by Barron and Darling-Hammond, for example, claims that *'decades of research illustrate the benefits of inquiry-based and cooperative learning to help students develop the knowledge and skills necessary to be successful in a rapidly changing world'* (2008, p 3). This claim significantly overstates the evidence, and conflates domains where you might expect high levels of mastery with every educational domain. Problem-based learning, for example, emerged out of medical school training programmes where the learners are likely to be highly academically successful already. If the cognitive scientists are correct, and enquiry learning can only work with students who already have some mastery of the domain, then we would expect these strategies to be less effective with younger or less experienced learners. In addition, there are more likely to be collaborative issues with younger learners as they lack the self-regulation and social skills necessary to learn with effectiveness in a group.

Don't expect students to be teachers

The Education Endowment Foundation (2017c) note *that 'peer tutoring appears to be particularly effective when pupils are provided with support to ensure that the quality of peer interaction is high… Peer tutoring appears to be less effective when the approach replaces normal teaching, rather than supplementing or enhancing it.'* Similarly, peer feedback tasks require teachers to strike a balance between empowering students and overwhelming them. Nelson and Schunn (2009a) argue that any effective model of peer feedback needs to teach the students what good feedback looks like and give them practice in delivering effective feedback. Understanding error and giving feedback are two different skills and teachers need to be careful as weakness in either leads to ineffective peer learning. Liu and Carless (2006) suggest that good peer feedback fulfils the following criteria.

- **It generally doesn't use grades.** Students cannot be expected to assess with the expertise and precision of teachers. Assigning grades can be meaningless and distracting.

- **It focuses feedback on learning.** Students should use peer feedback to make learning visible to themselves and their peers, and in doing so be able to develop awareness of what they need to do to improve.

- **It is regular, simple and focused.** Students need simple frameworks for offering feedback as they cannot cope with full assessment rubrics. They also need to be practised in giving feedback and be expecting it as part of their classroom culture. Where peer marking is used, it should focus on overall mark criteria which are well understood by the students (Falchikov and Goldfinch, 2000).

Use collaborative and cooperative forms of learning in a targeted manner to focus on specific learning goals

Given the lack of evidence for the overall superiority of peer-based learning, you need to deploy it carefully.

- Until better evidence becomes available, **problem-based learning** should probably only be used in a few specific contexts, such as medical training. It should be used with knowledgeable individuals where the focus of the task is complex problem-solving and acquiring other qualities such as building team cohesion or cognitive resilience.

- **Cooperative and collaborative learning** work, but only if appropriately designed and should probably be used in conjunction with individual modes of learning when the task is relatively difficult. They are particularly relevant when there are highly specific secondary goals in mind, such as building higher-level thinking skills or developing social relationships. Teachers need to think carefully about the individual learning achieved by any task and should not mistake group success for evidence of individual learning.

Structuring the task effectively is the key to effective peer learning

Peer learning that replaces teacher expertise with open-ended group-learning tasks will fail simply because students lack the expertise that would come from the direction of a teacher. Students can spread ignorance just as easily as knowledge, and can rapidly lose focus or waste cognitive effort on the wrong things. However, if properly structured, the evidence shows that collaborative and cooperative modes can work. In this context, structure means:

- clear roles for participants;

- clear goals and mechanisms for communication;

- appropriate scaffolds from the teacher to support and direct learning;

- a framework for group learning.

Lange et al (2016, p 260) conclude that the more student-centred the learning is, the more rigorous the task design needs to be, noting that *'more developed and structured group tasks improve the overall learning experience of group work'*. Assessment design should seek to remove any cognitive burdens or dead ends so that students can focus their working memories on the learning task. Similarly, it is critical that group-learning tasks are built with an element of individual accountability. Without an element of individual accountability, the drive to collaborate can be weakened and the benefits of group learning can be lost (Morgan, 1994; Williams et al, 2005; Laal et al, 2013).

6.4 Summary

Interactive forms of learning present a real assessment dilemma for teachers. The evidence suggests that there are benefits to group learning, but measuring and using those effects via assessment is tricky. While peer learning opens many new assessment options, its superiority as a strategy for imparting knowledge is not clear, particularly for novice learners. Its claims of superior efficacy rest on its overall efficacy as a teaching strategy, including its secondary benefits such as social learning, student motivation and communication skills. Certain forms of social learning do seem to be more effective than others. Peer learning and tutoring both seem to be particularly effective, mainly because they can be used to stimulate formative reflection on assessment. There is such a mixed picture of evidence for the efficacy of problem-based learning and other forms of project-based learning, but it may be possible to get effective learning through scaffolding that is aware of the cognitive challenge of learning in groups.

Questions for enquiry in your own school

- How and where do you use peer learning? What is the rationale for its use?

- Do you make careful use of scaffolds and instructions when you are setting group work?

- To what extent do you support students by giving them frameworks for peer feedback?

Exploring further

There are excellent summaries of peer feedback and mentoring, as well as links to evidence, on the Education Endowment Foundation website. Peer learning is also explored in considerable detail in Chapter 6 of Dylan Wiliam's *Embedded Formative Assessment* (2011). For a great discussion of the problems of peer learning and peer research, Kirschner et al's (2009) paper 'A Cognitive-Load Approach to Collaborative Learning' is an excellent summary.

- Wiliam, D (2011) *Embedded Formative Assessment*. Bloomington, IN: Solution Tree Press.

- Kirschner, F, Paas, F and Kirschner, P A (2009) A Cognitive Load Approach to Collaborative Learning: United Brains for Complex Tasks. *Educational Psychology Review*, 21: 31–42.

Chapter 7
Assessment and curriculum design

7.1 Chapter overview

This chapter will outline:

7.2   key ideas about assessment and curriculum design;

7.3   what the evidence says about assessment and curriculum design.

7.2 Key ideas

So far in this book, you have learnt what formative assessment is and how it relates to the cognitive systems that underpin learning. In this chapter, we will examine models for assessment that bring all these elements together in effective curriculum design.

The introduction of the national curriculum in 1988 led to controversy about the degree of independence teachers have to control what they teach. One recurrent criticism was that by specifying a national curriculum, it removed the power of teachers to develop their own curriculum. The truth is that even within a national curriculum, schools have enormous control over what and how they teach. It is perhaps useful, therefore, to make a distinction between curriculum in the national sense, and curriculum in its pedagogical sense, meaning *'all the learning which is planned and guided by the school, whether it is carried on in groups or individually, inside or outside the school'* (Kelly, 2004, p 7). It is this pedagogical definition which the word *curriculum* refers to when used in this chapter.

The decisions teachers make which can be considered as curriculum design decisions range from choosing the subject matter taught, to the choice of resources and how students are assessed. While there is an interesting debate to be had about the merits of extending or restricting the control teachers have over their curriculums, this is not one that we will be exploring in this book. Instead, it will be assumed that teachers are working within the structures of the UK national curriculum (or similar), and have a commensurate level of freedom to choose their own curriculum. Within these constraints, teachers actually have a lot of authority over issues of curriculum.

Table 7a Teacher decisions informed by curriculum design

Subject choice	Which subjects are carried by the institution?
Syllabus choice	Which syllabuses are chosen to be taught?
Course content choice	Which topics are covered within the course?
Lesson choice	How are the subjects taught in lessons?
Assessment choice	How does the teacher use assessment on the course?

It is, of course, the last of these which will be focused on in this chapter, but it is worth considering the relationship that assessment has to all of these other decisions. One fatalistic way of looking at it would be to say that because the summative assessment is fixed (Statutory Assessment Test (SATs)/General Certificate of Secondary Education (GCSEs)/Advanced Level (A levels) etc) then our assessment choices are limited, and by extension our lessons and course content. In practice, this is far from accurate, as the majority of assessment that will take place will be formative and thus central to preparing students for summative outcomes. In fact, the teacher has a huge range of assessment decisions to make, such as:

- the relationship between assessment and lesson planning;
- modes of assessment;
- questioning methods in class;
- how and when to test underlying knowledge;
- how and when to schedule full assessments;
- how to scaffold assessments;
- the role that peer or self-assessment plays in the assessment process;
- choosing how to include metacognitive elements in the assessment process.

The temptation is to see assessment as a by-product of curriculum design, but the evidence suggests that the relationship is far more integrated than that. Given the central role that assessment has in driving learning, teachers must see assessment as an integrated and central factor in their long-term and day-to-day planning. A formative mode of practice requires teachers to think not in terms of topics covered, but in terms of **models of progression**.

Models of progression

Figure 7a A simple model of progression in modern foreign languages

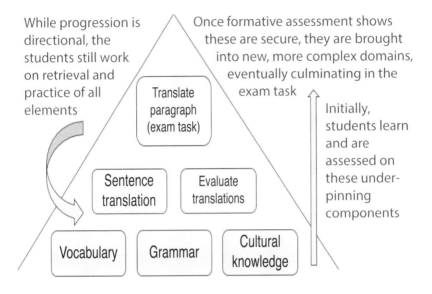

While progression is directional, the students still work on retrieval and practice of all elements

Once formative assessment shows these are secure, they are brought into new, more complex domains, eventually culminating in the exam task

Translate paragraph (exam task)

Initially, students learn and are assessed on these under-pinning components

Sentence translation

Evaluate translations

Vocabulary

Grammar

Cultural knowledge

Given the increasingly accountability-driven nature of assessment, summative forms of assessment tend to occupy the minds of teachers more than formative forms. The relationship between summative goals and formative assessment is not always clear. To fix this, both Wiliam (2011) and Christodoulou (2017) discuss the idea of *models of progression*, hierarchical structures of knowledge and skills which integrate the curriculum with assessment, reflection and planning. Individual components of learning may be significantly different in nature from an eventual summative task. For example, to complete the difficult task of writing a translation of a paragraph from English into French, the teacher may need to plan a sequential series of tasks in which very few of them are actually the final skill of translation until near the end of the learning journey. Students will likely need to acquire vocabulary, grammar knowledge, small-scale translation skills and even cultural knowledge to complete a specific whole-paragraph translation task. Within each model of progression, formative assessment is the tool by which a teacher can successfully guide and reinforce the learning of a student. Crucially, models of progression are highly domain-dependent and what they look like is contingent upon what knowledge or skills are being acquired. The goal of a model of progression is not to make students good at an examination task (this should occur as a natural by-product of an effective model of progression) but **to progress effectively through a curriculum**. This is a substantial shift from entirely summative-focused models of learning, and requires teachers to focus on the progression of learning instead of the progression of outcomes. To aid understanding, look at Figure 7a for a visualisation of a model of progression in modern foreign languages.

Cognitive load theory and models of progression

The idea of **models of progression** requires us to revisit the idea of **cognitive load theory** that we encountered in Chapter 4. This is the theory which states that the working memory is the narrow space that gives access to the long-term memory, and that effective management of cognitive load is critical to effective learning. Failure in a task is due to cognitive overload, and the only effective way that a teacher can prevent cognitive failure is to increase the quality and quantity of relevant schemas that a student has in long-term memory. Once a student has more knowledge, they can begin to use these resources in tasks and problem-solving, drawing upon long-term memory (which is vast and which does not create additional cognitive burden when used) rather than trying to rely upon limited working memory. Models of progression are designed to slowly build the necessary schemas of knowledge that we need to make progress towards a difficult goal. They link formative assessment to summative assessment in a practical way. They force a teacher to think through how they can use assessment to most effectively build schemas of knowledge in their students' heads.

7.3 What does the evidence say?

Cognitive load and curriculum design

Cognitive load is a biological constraint which has the greatest impact upon curriculum design (if you wish to revisit the definition or the evidence for its existence, then please go back to Chapter 4). Here the focus will be on the implications of cognitive load theory and how it impacts curriculum design. As Kirschner explains, '*the limitations of working memory are rarely taken into account in conventional instruction*' (2002, p 2), meaning that curriculum design tends to presume that students have flexible and expansive working memories, when in fact working memory is extremely limited. Schemes of work often conceive of learning as a sequence of topics, presuming learning to just happen when teacher and student cover a topic together. Cognitive load theory shows how complex and constrained learning actually is. Unnecessary burden on working memory is counterproductive to effective learning, and teachers should therefore remember the following guidelines when designing assessments within their curriculum:

Table 7b Principles of assessment design using cognitive load theory

Begin with small steps	At the beginning of learning a new task, learners don't have the schemas in long-term memory to succeed at cognitively complex tasks. Failure on summative assessment tasks at this stage will tell you very little. Assess low-level components to reinforce key knowledge in memory and start building towards more complex elements.
Provide scaffolds and worked examples to reduce cognitive load	Scaffolds and worked examples are important for helping students build appropriate schemas of knowledge. Scaffolded assessments reduce cognitive load on working memory, and allow teachers to direct resources on relevant areas. Worked examples allow students to see and store relevant schemas for future problem-solving.
Reduce extraneous load	Extraneous load can be *environmental* (classroom noise, students talking, tiredness) or *built into the task* itself (poor assessment design, poor choice of task, etc). Make sure that what students are thinking about is what is relevant, and nothing else. One good strategy to achieve this would be to reduce the number of sources of information, or to condense multiple sources into single sources.
Design assessments that have the right level of *desirable difficulty*	Tasks will have an intrinsic load, but the very best will make appropriate use of germane load as well. Make assessment too hard, and students will experience cognitive failure and thus learn nothing. But if the assessment is too easy, your students are so scaffolded that they will not have to exert themselves and therefore acquire deep learning. Be prepared to let students struggle a little, provided it is managed correctly.
Review and repeat to build schemas of knowledge	Learning knowledge or solving a problem just once leaves little impact on long-term memory. Successful completion of an assessment tells you little about long-term retention. You must plan for repetition and practice to be able to see performance turn into learning in your assessments.

Encourage the use of imag-ination and self-explanation in solving assessments	*Imagining solutions to problems* and *explaining solutions to yourself or a partner* are cognitively effective tools for building effective schemas, as they require students to rehearse ideas.

Knowledge and assessment design

Building models of progression for learning shows the importance of planned formative assessment of knowledge. Knowledge is domain-specific, and for students to improve their skills in that domain, they need to improve their knowledge. This also holds true for assessment. For example, questioning that is not generic has a greater impact upon learning (Rosenshine and Meister, 1994). Critically, this means regularly assessing knowledge is a fundamental part of a model of progression. Some good principles of knowledge assessment design are as follows:

- **Have a clear sense of the relevance and order of the knowledge you are teaching.** Which concepts are predicated upon secure knowledge of other concepts? How essential is each piece of knowledge?

- **Interleave learning and recall for maximum effect.** Recalling and extend-ing topics should be an ongoing process, not two frantic weeks of revision at the end.

- **Practise the power of forgetting**, and leave gaps between learning and incidents of recall to ensure that students make effortful attempts to recall, and thus strengthen, memory.

- **Prepare concrete examples on which to hang key ideas.** Good metaphors/analogies/mnemonics are effective for framing the concepts in memory.

- **Use visualisations and encourage students to create visualisations** to make use of the dual coding effect to build better memories (Mayer and Anderson, 1991).

- **Reduce key ideas to their most useable forms**, and in some cases embrace the fact that there will be several distinct stages of knowledge acquisition as they begin to develop and link the concept to other forms of learning.

- **Anticipate errors in understanding.** Look at what concepts students have struggled with before and plan better instruction and assessment to meet that challenge.

- **Remember the importance *of cognitive elaboration*** and plan in advance how the core knowledge is going to be extended and connected with other knowledge. Assessment is critical here. Do you extend via specific tasks or deliberate questioning?

Deliberate practice and assessment design

Deliberate practice is one of the more valuable concepts that have emerged from cognitive science, and it is associated with the work of Ericsson (2006, 2008, 2016). His research has shown how the performance of experts, while often seemingly effortless and intuitive, is in fact usually the result of many hours of careful practice. When we see a master performing in a domain at a very high level, there is a huge pyramid of underpinning skills and knowledge that have been deliberately practised, over and over. It must be noted that blind repetition isn't what is being described here. The notion of *deliberate* practice emphasises the importance of ensuring the practice is relevant, focused and guided by experts. Crucially, this shows a critical relationship between deliberate practice and assessment; it is only through formative assessment that a teacher can identify the most effective areas for further practice. The idea of deliberate practice is not without controversy. Firstly, it has often been misinterpreted in a simplified form, appearing in pop culture thanks to Malcolm Gladwell (2009) as the 10,000 hour rule. This number has been challenged by Ericsson himself, who stressed that there is a lot of variability in the exact number of hours that leads to mastery, but evidence remains that practice correlates with performance across a wide range of domains.

In recent years there have been some studies which have suggested that deliberate practice may be less potent than had previously been claimed. One meta-analysis concluded that *'amount of deliberate practice—although unquestionably important as a predictor of individual differences in performance from both a statistical and a practical perspective—is not as important as Ericsson and his colleagues have argued'* (Macnamara et al, 2014, p 1617). This meta-analysis also explored the idea that variance in deliberate practice was because of other factors, such as motivation or talent. For example, children will work harder on things that they find easy. However, others have argued that all that really has been found are confounding factors, not evidence that practice itself is without value (Hambrick et al, 2007). Student success is probably a combination of both deliberate practice and these other factors, meaning it is still a tool that can and should be leveraged in the classroom. It is fair to say though, that the extent to which we can conceive of practice as being distinct from raw intelligence or talent is unclear.

So how does deliberate practice affect assessment design? Christodoulou (2017) suggests that the deliberate nature of practice makes assessment invaluable. We can only know where strengths and weaknesses exist through assessment.

Without assessment, deliberate practice is guesswork. Critically, as well, assessment *is* practice when used deliberately. Whether as rehearsal for the final assessment, or in a model of progression, practice is an underpinning element of the final skill.

7.4 Summary

Teachers make a lot of choices about what the curriculum is, and how it might be implemented. An understanding of the key evidence can make those decisions far more effective. Probably the most important concept to understand in effective curriculum design is that of **cognitive load**. Working memory is the narrow resource that permits access to long-term memory, and curriculum design must work within its constraints to produce effective and deep learning. Well-designed assessments are a critical tool for helping students manage cognitive load effectively and they should promote learning, not merely performance on tests. In curriculum design, the most useful way to envision the relationship between summative and formative assessment is the idea of a **model of progression**. This suggests that we should be focusing not on the progress towards a final summative assessment, but the learning that moves students through the academic domain itself. One result of this shift in emphasis is that what is assessed in the classroom often doesn't look like the final assessment, particularly at the start of the learning process.

Questions for enquiry in your own school

- What decisions do you personally make about curriculum design?
- Do you plan to avoid cognitive overload in the early stages of your curriculum design?
- What would a model of progression look like in your subject?

Exploring further

For an accessible introduction to cognitive load theory, read Paul Kirschner's paper 'Cognitive Load Theory: Implications of Cognitive Load Theory on the Design of Learning' (2002).

- Kirschner, P A (2002) Cognitive Load Theory: Implications of Cognitive Load Theory on the Design of Learning. *Learning and Instruction*, 12: 1–10.

For a discussion of models of progression and formative assessment in curriculum design, then read Daisy Christodoulou's excellent book *Making Good Progress?* (2017).

- Christodoulou, D (2017) *Making Good Progress? The Future of Assessment for Learning*. New ed. Oxford: Oxford University Press.

Chapter 8
How has assessment been most effectively implemented?

8.1 Chapter overview

This chapter will outline:

8.2 key ideas and examples of effective implementation of assessment;

8.3 what the evidence says about effective implementation of assessment.

8.2 Key ideas and examples

As this book has now explored all the important elements of assessment, it is now time to consider what has been learnt when assessment has been implemented in the real world. There is a surprising amount of research already on the implementation of assessment in schools, but it is far from complete. However, there is more than enough to draw some conclusions – the most important of which has been to highlight the role of professional development and educational culture in supporting change. The emerging consensus is that a model of a self-improving school network seems the most effective way to create sustained, effective change.

What do studies into implementation look like?

There are two major sources of research into implementation:

1. **Qualitative reviews of large-scale implementations.** These have the advantage of being large but lack the rigour of formal experiments. As such, they offer a lot of interesting reflection and insight, but can be poor at giving evidence of specific effects.

2. **Small-scale research projects.** These are more specific in their interventions and effects, and often include relatively small numbers of students and teachers in their designs.

These two sources can often be the same thing, as small-scale research projects are often part of pilot implementations that go on to be instituted more widely, leading to qualitative review data. The major gap in the evidence is for large-scale (ie hundreds of schools) studies of implementation which have rigorous experimental design, such as control groups. The main barrier to these kinds of studies is the sheer complexity of running these experiments. Not just the simple logistics, but also the difficulty of applying experimental controls at scale. Without a body of studies of this kind of scale and rigour, we cannot conduct the kinds of meta-analyses we have seen in areas such as peer learning. However, this does not mean that we cannot draw any valid conclusions from the existing evidence.

Global analysis of implementation

The best sources for large-scale implementation data is probably the Organisation for Economic Co-operation and Development (OECD), which has looked in detail at formative assessment across the world. In Table 8a you can see examples of some of the major implementations of assessment reform from across the world.

Table 8a International implementation of formative assessment (OECD and beyond)

Country	Implementation
Australia (Queensland)	Each state or territory has control over its own school system, although nationwide initiatives have also been brought in. Queensland has implemented assessment initiatives in relation to these.
Canada	A variety of AfL initiatives, varying on a province-by-province basis, with some coordination by national agencies.
Denmark	Formative assessment is not systematically implemented throughout Denmark, although the education ministry is responsible for providing tools and implementing assessments. Higher education was the main research focus for the OECD's *Improving Teaching and Learning for Adults with Basic Skill Needs through Formative Assessment* research project (Baltzer and Colardyn, 2006).
England	Has been developed through several national formative assessment initiatives, starting with the publication of Black and Wiliam's review (1998b) and through subsequent national policies. There remains no fixed national standards for delivery.

Finland	Operates a policy of centralised steering but local implementation. National policies place a focus on assessment for evaluation, not competition. Individual school responsible for implementation.
Italy	The national assessment structure has implemented formative reforms since 2003.
New Zealand	Formative assessment is not a single national policy, but is embedded in various other initiatives on curriculum and examinations.
Norway	Has put into law the students' right to formative assessment. The Norwegian schools system increasingly makes use of assessment and the Norwegian Directorate for Education and training has developed a national programme.
Scotland	Has had various assessment initiatives in place since the early 1990s, but these have had some mixed success. The *Assessment is for Learning* programme (AifL) was put in place in 2002.
Singapore	Has had a programme of assessment reform since 1997, trying to increasingly inject formative assessment into a powerfully summative culture.

Formative assessment as a tool for professional development

Studies into the implementation of assessment reform have shown a powerful overlap between assessment and teacher training. When used to reflect and review, assessment can be an outstanding tool for professional development. As we have seen in previous chapters, good assessment is predicated upon deep professional knowledge such as:

- rich subject knowledge;
- knowledge of effective strategies to teach complex skills within the domain;
- knowledge of common errors of understanding within the domain;
- knowledge of the stickiness and difficulty of key ideas;
- knowledge of students and their limitations.

Formative assessment is the most powerful tool available to acquire this kind of knowledge. By reviewing and reflecting upon assessment, teachers can build deep knowledge of their subject and their craft (Wiliam, 2016). On the back of this, robust, lasting institutional change can be built.

8.3 What does the evidence say?

Evidence on implementing assessment remains very diffuse. Very few studies have the robustness of design of a randomised controlled trial (RCT), but the qualitative studies do often have the advantage having very large cohorts of students involved. There is lots of great information here, but we need to proceed with caution. The key issues are that:

- Evidence on the implementation of formative assessment is drawn from a wide range of disparate sources.

- There is not yet sufficient evidence for a robust meta-analysis into assessment as there is too much variance in the concepts being applied and in the local conditions under which they take place. Attempts to draw a firm conclusion about effect size are similarly limited.

Despite these limitations, there is a lot of useful data in the studies that do exist. From these, it is possible to draw the following conclusions about implementing assessment reform:

Implementing formative change is hard in a summative world

The most prominent fact that studies of assessment implementation reveal is how much education systems across the world are still trapped between formative and summative assessment needs. Education systems can be high-performing without much focus on formative assessment. An example is Singapore, which in the past has relied on high volumes of summative assessment combined with private tuition and cultural expectation to drive achievement (Lim and Tan, 1999). In comparison, Finland has historically been a high-performing country, and it rates summative outcomes as only the fourth most important function of assessment, focusing instead upon using assessment to reflect upon learning (Voogt and Kasurinen, 2005).

The main conclusion to draw from international comparisons is that cultural context matters for implementation of assessment changes. Initially, Singapore had relatively little success in implementing formative assessment due to structural resistance from parents and teachers (Leong and Tan, 2014; Ratnam-Lim and Tan, 2015). The value of formative assessment was poorly understood, whereas summative grades were so highly valued that they prevented formative feedback from being properly understood. In high-stakes summative cultures, assessment reform requires the buy-in of all stakehold-ers, particularly other teachers in the institution, students and parents. These are problems likely to be encountered by all teachers working within similarly rigid accountability structures. Similarly, the individual comparisons reveal the differences between systems focused on centralised control, and those which devolve decisions on assessment to teachers. The best implementations manage to negotiate a careful path between control and flexibility. There is a temptation to impose a top-down, systematic approach to change in order to drive change to take place, but this often comes at the cost of teachers taking ownership. As Lee and Wiliam (2005, p 265) explain:

to be most effective, teacher professional development needs to be structured strongly enough to afford teacher growth, but flexible enough to allow different teachers to take their practice in different ways.

Changing teachers' practice is hard

Across all the implementation studies, one consistent barrier to change is the inertia of teachers against change to their practice. System-wide changes such as assessment calendars and team-led data reviews are relatively clear and manageable changes, but adopting a formative mode of practice entails *'chang-ing habits, ingrained, for many teachers, over years and sometimes decades'* (Wiliam, 2016, p 185). Even new teachers have experience of the classroom as students, which can set their expectations to less productive modes. We must under-stand the psychological dimensions of change when implementing reform, or we can inadvertently create the conditions for failure.

Decisions about teaching are not necessarily rational; in fact, they are far more likely to be intuitive and emotional. The brain erects complex defences against new ideas that clash with deeply held beliefs (Nyhan and Reifler, 2010). Avoid-ing defensiveness against evidence and ideas requires leaders of change to strip information down to core facts, clearly challenge incorrect assumptions and provide clear alternative explanations for why evidence-based forms of assessment are accurate (Cook and Lewandowsky, 2011). Facts by themselves will struggle to be accepted without addressing these emotional dimensions, as the KMOFAP project noted *'where educational research is concerned, the facts do not necessarily speak for themselves'* (Black and Wiliam, 2005, p 236). Wiliam (2016) suggests a set of principles, drawing heavily upon the work of Heath and Heath (2011) among others, to maximise the chance that change will take effect:

Table 8b Principles that positively affect changes to school systems, adapted from Wiliam (2016, pp 185–205)

Principle	Explanation	Practical examples
Focus on existing success and build upon it	Change doesn't have to be something entirely new. Even schools in special measures will have pockets of good assessment practice within them. These need to be protected and nurtured. Change that seeks to sweep away everything has no bedrock for future growth.	Use teachers with good practice to lead change; they are often more credible persuaders. Use existing forms of assessment that are effective and popular as the model for future innovation.
Script the critical moves	When broken down into clear steps and carefully walked through, change is far less intimidating and much easier to grasp and accept.	Structural change in assessment should focus on clear, simultaneous changes in components of the assessment system. Provide meaningful changes that teachers can understand and implement rather than vague commands to 'do better assessment'.
Point to the desti-nation	Without an overt, clear destination in mind, the competing ideas about professional practice can overwhelm attempts at progress on assessment.	Leadership that wants to see change must be specific about how to measure success of that change from the outset.
Lever-age the emotional appeal	The most powerful driver of change is a change of heart in teachers. Emotional, intuitive appeals open the drawbridge to more factual, detailed arguments.	Make emotionally intuitive arguments first, such as the desire to help pupils, or the moral imperative to improve standards, before jumping to evidence and studies.

Make change manageable	Given most teachers' comfort with existing teaching methods, presenting them with a vast set of changes is likely to cause them to balk and make change fail before it has even got started.	While still pointing to a clear final goal, present initial changes that are reasonable and intuitive.
Maintain a growth mindset for all	Teachers must be persuaded of the capacity for change, and that they are able to grow themselves.	Finding leaders of change allows you to grow them as individuals. Similarly, decoupling change from performance management systems can better frame change as being for change's sake.
Tweak the path	Change is an ongoing dialogue, not just a linear process. Effective change must respond to success and failure as it happens.	Good leaders show the capacity for change, model the change in their own behaviour and offer opportunities for discussion of the change itself.
Build effective habits	Short-term change can be driven by authoritative changes and restrictive processes, but true change emerges from long-term adjustments in habits and assumptions.	Failure to change habits is often caused by people abandoning a course of action in the face of failure or challenge. Decide in advance on 'action triggers' – what will happen with each given outcome – which will help maintain momentum when encountering resistance to change.
Rally the herd	Creating *a group ethos around cultural practices* (Wiliam, 2016, p 200) helps to institutionalise change and make it easier.	Use of slogans and mnemonics to collectivise ideas. Invite discussion of institutional principles. Frame changes as being the 'way' of the institution.

Change can only be seen through if the right environment is created

The studies have been remarkably consistent when it comes to identifying the kind of school culture that can make assessment reform effective and permanent. The key factors that lead to success are:

Making time

One common issue that is mentioned across the studies is the challenge of finding time to adequately complete the work. Indeed, the impact of formative assessment upon workload was a common fear encountered by researchers when they tried to take it into the classroom (Hopfenbeck et al, 2015). 'Bolt-on' approaches to formative assessment – those that treat it as a nice optional extra, as opposed to a fundamental shift in practice – can easily add to workload and be rejected. Time for planning and reflecting assessment should be seen as a priority and an important investment.

Collaboration

Collaborative approaches to implementation are generally more effective than top-down, systematic approaches (Black and Wiliam, 2005; Hopfenbeck and Stobart, 2015). Collaboration helps all parties. In large-scale implementations, researchers and government agencies are better able to manage implementation when they have listened closely to classroom teachers. The teachers themselves are more likely to be engaged and less afraid if they feel part of the process of devising the assessment intervention. For example, van den Berg et al (2016) stress the negative impact that a lack of clarity can have on a formative assessment intervention. In their study, they focused on giving collaborative planning time to establish a working model for the intervention. Their four-stage model sought to strike a balance between expert knowledge and teacher ownership.

Table 8c Four-stage model, adapted from van den Berg et al (2016)

Phase 1	Researchers and curriculum experts	Defined the problem and reviewed research relevant to the problem to create a concept of the formative assessment model.
Phase 2	Researchers and teachers	Developed the classroom formative assessment with a small group of teachers including peer observation and evaluation.
Phase 3	Researchers and teachers	Refined the model based upon formative reflection and evaluation.
Phase 4	Researchers and teachers	Implemented the prototype model repeatedly, with analysis and reflection, to refine it further.

Of course, not all institutions are lucky enough to have support from universities to guide implementation. This has increasingly led to calls for more school–university research partnerships, where two-way learning can take place between academics and practitioners in the classroom (Cornelissen et al, 2011). While there are many ideological and practical issues with making research partnerships work (McLaughlin et al, 2006) in the long run, these forms of institutional collaboration may provide more secure foundations for assessment reform. The extent to which these involve the teacher as an active researcher, however, is unclear.

Mentoring and leadership
One conclusion that has been drawn across different studies is the importance of effective mentorship throughout the process. Black and Wiliam (2005, p 236) concluded that it was only the presence of experienced teachers with deep subject knowledge that allowed the KMOFAP project to be effective. Without the credibility of the trainers, the interventions could have been seen as supplementary and redundant. Leaders need to be both subject experts and fully versed in a formative mode of practice for them to drive change effectively. Teachers also need a balance between effective structures and freedom to explore and make mistakes. Ideally, teachers need *a school-wide culture that facilitates collaboration and encourages teacher autonomy'* (Heitink et al, 2016, p 50).

Reflection

Changes to assessment can cause significant change to the professional lives of teachers and their students. It can be *'a tacit process'* (Bell and Cowie, 2001a, p 547) that can *'change the rules, usually implicit, that govern the behaviours that are expected and seen as legitimate by teachers and by students'* (Black and Wiliam, 2005, p 234). As such, teachers need time and space to reflect upon these changes, or else the sense of disruption can outweigh any other positives. We can see an example of this in the KMOFAP project where teachers viewed grading papers as an irreducible aspect of teaching, and initially reacted with shock and surprise when presented with research evidence which contradicted this preconception. However, when they began to experience the strategy for themselves, the new strategy proved popular:

> **Potential conflicts with school policy were resolved as experience showed that the provision of comments gave both students and their parents advice on how to improve. It also set up a new focus on the learning issues rather than on trying to interpret a mark or grade.**
>
> (Black and Wiliam, 2005, p 230)

Similarly, Antoniou and James (2014) found that teachers were surprised by the fact that much of formative assessment is unplanned. This clashed with preconceptions of formative assessment being planned and systematic, and led some teachers to experience doubts about the validity of the changes. In situations such as this, reflection time is critical to allow teachers to cope with these responses and give them a chance to explore and work through them. As part of this process, it may be helpful to develop a common language of formative assessment (Bell and Cowie, 2001b, p 47).

8.4 Summary

While the evidence is quite diverse, there are things that effective assessment interventions have in common:

- They anticipate and prepare for resistance to change. This requires awareness of the barriers to change and carefully crafted messages.

- They work with the experience of the teaching group, using a collaborative approach and knowledgeable, understanding leadership.

- They make sure the process is reflective and that suitable time and resources are made available for this.

- What is the culture regarding improvement? Is there acceptance of experimentation and failure?

- What are the mechanisms for collaboration within your school?

- Do senior leaders have a good knowledge of formative assessment?

- Is enough time made available for reflection and planning?

Exploring further

For a superb, detailed discussion of implementing change, read Dylan Wiliam's book *Leadership for Teaching Learning*. This covers the issues discussed here in much greater detail.

- Wiliam, D (2016) *Leadership for Teacher Learning: Creating a Culture Where All Teachers Improve So That All Students Succeed.* West Palm Beach, FL: Learning Sciences International.

Chapter 9
Putting assessment into practice

9.1 Chapter overview

This chapter will outline:

9.2 how you can prepare for implementation;

9.3 how you measure success;

9.4 key actions required;

9.5 the assessment debate revisited;

9.6 what good assessment is.

9.2 How do I prepare for implementation?

'Nothing works everywhere and everything works somewhere' is the mantra suggested by Dylan Wiliam in regard to evidence-based approaches to education (2013, p 13). This seems to offer little hope of a universal intervention for improving assessment, but the evidence explored in Chapters 7 and 8 does point to a methodology. Now that this book has walked through the evidence on assessment, it would now be useful to reflect on what this means for implementation in your own school or college, particularly if you are going to assemble a coherent approach that minimises the risk of creating a failed intervention. To this end, this chapter looks at the essential questions to ask and the methodologies which are most likely to lead to success. Turning evidence into practice is probably the hardest step of all. Careful planning and appropriate expectations are essential. Quick-fire solutions and broad approaches are likely to be ineffective as they make it difficult to pinpoint effective change.

What questions should be asked?

The most important question at the start of the process is: *What am I seeking to achieve?* Without first considering what the destination is, it is very easy to get lost in the process. Be clear and pragmatic about the goal, or else the project can rapidly spiral out of control and it can unnecessarily feel like a failure. The answers to this question should be specific, achievable and measurable. The Education Endowment Foundation has made a lot of resources to support teachers who are exploring evidence-based approaches. In their *DIY Evaluation Guide* (2017a) they suggest that a good research question should be phrased as follows

I would really like to know if _____ **(intervention)**
would have an impact on _____ **(outcome) in (our school).**

This structure forces the teacher to think about specific outcomes, while also being specific about the target group and context. An effective research question might look like this:

I would really like to know if greater use of in-class formative assessment techniques would have an impact on GCSE English results in St Catherine's High School.

Critically, whatever your answer to the question _what am I seeking to achieve_? you must specify what it is you are evaluating, what outcome you will measure and the context it will be taking place in.

How do I choose the right intervention?

As has been previously suggested in Chapter 7, the most holistic model of assessment available is probably some version of a **model of progression**. Depending upon the school context or the planning time available, implementing this idea in its entirety may or may not be feasible. In many cases, it may be preferable to implement some smaller aspect of that model in the form of an assessment intervention. This would take the form of a structured change in assessment practice with a desired outcome and meaningful way of measuring impact. Assessment interventions may have several stages or components but, broadly speaking, there are two ways you can change practice:

1. Improving the quality of the assessment itself.

2. Making existing assessment more formative.

Clearly, 1 and 2 overlap, but they are listed separately here because it is possible to implement them individually. For example, we can leverage the power of assessment to improve memory by bringing in new quizzes and tests without necessarily using that data formatively. However, it is clearly advisable to make use of all the power for improvement that assessment makes available. Any effective intervention may well change both.

Table 9a Examples of interventions

1. Improving the quality of the assessments themselves	• Designing more valid assessments or improving the validity of existing assessments. • Improving the reliability of marking. • Introducing new tools for assessment. • Making assessments better at assessing the desired outcomes.
2. Making assessment more formative	• Using existing formal assessments in a summative way. • Adopting a formative mode of practice in relation to classroom quizzes – using results to determine content on future tests. • Establishing data analysis teams to reflect on formal assessments. • Making students reflect on feedback in lesson time.

One thing that should be clear from reading the previous chapters is that isolated interventions around assessment tend not to work. In planning a change in you or your team's practice, you need to be aware of the tension between local change and the wider institutional culture. Local changes which fly in the face of cultural support factors tend to become isolated and die off. The specific intervention needs to be clear, but it needs to be planned with an awareness of the broader mechanisms of change (Cartwright and Hardie, 2012).

Table 9b The relationship between interventions and support factors

Example intervention	Support factors
Respond to scheduled assessments with intervention panels to review results	Do teachers understand why interventions are taking place? Is there sufficient time planned to reflect on its efficacy? Do teachers know what to look for?
Introduction of mini whiteboards as assessment tool	Do teachers understand what formative assessment means? Do teachers how to use this tool forma-tively? Are sufficient mini whiteboards available?

Posing questions of the student instead of offering comments when giving students feedback	Do teachers understand the value of this strategy? Do they know what an effective question looks like? Will they know how to measure its impact?

Choosing an assessment intervention emerges out of a clear goal, an awareness of what things can make assessment better and an awareness of the wider contextual change that might be required to unlock its effects. The questions listed in Table 9c below should help you to choose the right intervention.

Planning your intervention

Table 9c Key questions to ask when planning your intervention

Key questions	Explanation
Are my expectations reasonable?	Few interventions, if any, will have a miraculous effect on outcomes. Change tends to happen slowly, and without easily measurable cause and effect. Keeping expectations reasonable will prevent you from getting disappointed and prevent you over-promising to colleagues.
Are the changes manageable and the intervention feasible?	In teaching, the greatest constraint on change is usually time. If the time cost is large, then no matter what the potential opportunity, change may be resisted and may be too unwieldy to implement. The same is also true of resource cost.
Does everyone involved have a clear understanding of the rationale?	Focusing on *how*, without explaining *why*, is likely to lead to failure. Firstly, teachers will have a strong understanding of why they use existing strategies and will likely resist strategies which they do not understand the point of. Secondly, without adequate understanding, they will not be able to implement the change effectively and therefore reject it as 'not working'.

Key questions	Explanation
What resources will I need?	Appropriate training resources are essential. These should be brief, manageable and directed at teachers. You may also need to think about assessment resources.

Assessment resources

One of the quickest ways for an intervention to fail is to not properly prepare suitable resources. While the additional burden it seems to place on teachers seems small, it won't take much for teachers to revert to their default practice. 'Resource' is quite a broad term as well, and can refer to the assessments themselves, but also to classroom tools that are used to support formative assessments, as well as the systems used to process data. A good rule of thumb is to never implement a system that you wouldn't be happy to use yourself. Keep it simple and always be aware of the time cost/benefit of any tool you introduce – there is often a desire to always use the most robust resource or process, when in many cases a less robust but quicker version may be better overall.

Table 9d Types of assessment resources

Assessment resource	Examples
Physical classroom tools	Whiteboards, egg-timers, students' folders, self-assessment cover sheets
Digital classroom tools	Electronic quizzing tools (Kahoot, Plickers etc), visualizers
Assessment management tools	Electronic mark books, cover sheets

9.3 How do I measure success?

Measuring success needs to be carefully managed to avoid overreach. The temptation can be to look so hard for measurable change that you end up distorting what is really happening. Similarly, pressure (whether internal or external) can create a need to get positive results, leading to unfounded perceptions of impact. Here are some good principles to follow if you want to appropriately frame changes to assessment for yourself and colleagues.

- **Discuss what will happen if no positive outcome is achieved.** This are the **action triggers** that were discussed in the previous chapter. You need to have carefully planned what your course of action is in the event of a null response. This way there is still a path to follow and you have also framed the possibility of failure.

- **Explain the methodology and process clearly in advance.** Have conversations with all stakeholders about what you are doing and the process you are taking part in.

- **Don't set expectations regarding success.** Frame all discussions in terms of enquiry, not possible gains. You are trying to find out what works for your school, not promise future riches.

Among the research community, there is little support for the idea of teachers becoming entirely driven by research. Wiliam (2014) has claimed that teaching will never be an entirely evidence-based profession. Instead, it is hoped that teachers may engage more in what might be termed 'disciplined enquiry', following a more rigorous and sceptical process than mere professional guesswork – informed by evidence but not restricted by it (Galdin-O'Shea, 2015). There should be no pressure to be a researcher; in fact, this goal is not even very realistic. We must be content to judge outcomes by less robust measures than professional education researchers have available.

One very valuable source of data is process data. This is the qualitative, reflective data that teachers receive from engaging in disciplined enquiry, and it forms much of the base of evidence for research into formative assessment. It consists of reflections on what is learned by taking part in the process, particularly implementation. Even if an intervention is entirely unsuccessful in terms of outcomes, the process data may be valuable. Taylor and Spence-Thomas (2015) suggest that this data can be collected in a range of ways, including surveys, questionnaires and lesson observation videos. This data also serves a secondary purpose of encouraging teachers to link the intervention to wider formative reflection on assessment.

Given the limits of experimental design in most school environments, there is very high risk of churning out junk data unless evaluation is carefully planned from the beginning. Teachers need to be aware of the following key points:

- Not all enquiry has to lead to measurable data outcomes. If the teachers are learning through reflection (ie generating process data) then this may be more than enough to explore the validity of an intervention.

- Teachers must plan measurement *in advance* of completing the intervention. Changing what is being measured, or how it is measured, midway through an intervention is a sure-fire way to bias the outcomes.

- Teachers need to measure a meaningful baseline if they wish to compare exam results. Students will make natural progress, regardless of the intervention, so an improvement in grades over the course of, for example, a single term, may have nothing to do with an intervention.

- Even if a measurable difference is found, be careful to not over-claim when other factors could also be responsible. It is very easy for those not trained in disciplined enquiry to misinterpret a measured improvement as a guaranteed, transferable improvement they can implement elsewhere. Make sure all stakeholders are aware of the limitations of the intervention study.

There is not enough space here to cover the permutations of experimental design and statistical measurement in much detail, suffice to say that unless you have some training or experience, it may be best to start in the more modest methodology of *disciplined enquiry.* If you wish to develop more robust methodologies it may be necessary to seek specialist training or to find academic partners.

9.4 Key actions

Long-term changes: becoming part of a learning community

Short-term change to assessment must always be viewed in the context of long-term changes in culture and pedagogy. One of the main conclusions that has emerged from classroom research into formative assessment has been the need for a wider institutional journey. The most profound change of all is to go from acting as an isolated teacher to being part of a Professional Learning Community (PLC) (Stoll et al, 2006; Vescio et al, 2008). In seeking change, you may find you have read more than your school leaders and that the assessment policy you work under is not based on evidence at all. It is therefore helpful to consider the things you can do to help grow the wider learning culture in your school as well.

Table 9e

Key action	Why is this important? / What is important?
Share accessible evidence-based assessment resources with other teachers	There have been a lot of attempts to make educational research accessible for teachers. Good examples are the Deans for Impact booklet *The Science of Learning* (2016) or *The Principles of Instruction* (Rosenshine, 2012), both of which contain a lot of relevant information about evidence-based approaches to assessment in condensed, accessible papers. Similarly, organisations like *ResearchEd* (www.workingoutwhatworks.com/) and *The Learning Scientists* (www.learningscientists.org/) have summary resources on a range of assessment topics. These are less intimidating than research papers and can often even be found in neat visualisations online.
Model evidence-based assessment techniques for peers	If you are prepared to show other teachers a practical example of evidence-based assessment practice, you have a much better chance of them understanding and implementing it. Observation and reflection with peers are very good tools for this.
Start a reading group	Although open-ended personal study tasks are usually not focused enough for impacting teacher behaviour, a structured reading group with a specific task and accessible resources may be a good way to engage teachers with evidence on assessment.
Attend a conference	The national ResearchEd conferences (www.workingoutwhatworks.com/) often have assessment streams and offer cheap, unparalleled opportunities to hear talks from the biggest names in the field. Similarly, many of the researchers mentioned in this book can be found at educational conferences.

Group planning	One of the simplest shifts that can have the most profound impact is to move to group planning and reflection. Once assessment is collaborative, it makes formative reflection almost impossible to avoid.
Assessment CPD	The best advocates for improvements to practice are other teachers. Only if we are willing to share practice and be the model for others can we expect change to spread. Remember, the evidence suggests that the only effective CPD is that which is sustained over two or more terms, and which is regular and relevant (Cordingley et al, 2015).
Use social media	Twitter is the preferred social media of much of the educational world. It offers unparalleled access to many of the most important figures in education, as well as linking you to a network of blogging practitioners who offer ideas and sounding boards for new assessment techniques.
Train an assessment lead	Durham University and Evidence-Based Education are now offering the first national training course for 'assessment leads'. These are designated assessment experts for their school, who undertake a training programme to get them to better understand the evidence on assessment.
Make time for reflection	This is a change that can only be made at a managerial level, but which still requires individual buy-in from teachers. Time must be planned and made available for teachers to reflect and plan future assessment. This time must be structured, focused and part of regular practice to become effective.

9.5 The assessment debate revisited

At the beginning of this book, it was suggested that the debate around assessment is so large that it can make it feel impossible to reach a meaningful conclusion about what impact it should have on your practice. Having read this book, the principles of good assessment should now hopefully be clear.

Assessment is a powerful tool because it causes relevant thought and recall, and this creates long-term learning. In addition, it can serve as an effective tool for inferring learning, thus allowing teachers to teach subsequent lessons better. Most powerfully of all, assessment is the basis for teachers' self-improvement, because it allows them to reflect on what works and what doesn't work.

Across the whole learning process, it can help a teacher build robust knowledge of the ways in which students learn and the ways they fail. In doing so, formative assessment is also the best bulwark against misplaced assumptions of efficacy that teachers frequently make about themselves.

However, assessment that is not implemented in a formative way can easily become assessment for assessment's sake. Equally, assessments that aren't set with thought and reflection can be very bad at making students think effectively. Teachers need to reflect on the evidence on assessment and have time and support to think about how to apply it to their practice.

9.6 What is good assessment?

Ultimately, all the research findings presented in this book boil down to three key principles:

Assessment is the engine that drives effective learning

Most of the time, assessment *is* learning. Assessment forces students to think and remember in relevant ways, and the assessment within a lesson or module is usually where learning is taking place. Without structured assessment, instruction leads to passivity or overload. Properly handled, assessment is the primary tool by which students can be made to build the mental structures that are essential for increasing and improving what students can do.

Assessment should be used by both teachers and students to reflect on learning

To maximise the impact of assessment, teachers need to have an opportunity to reflect and respond to it. Formative assessment is a reflective mode of practice, not a series of tweaks or tricks that can be imposed upon teachers from above. Developing that mode of practice requires knowledge, support and patience. Improving assessment is therefore a collaborative effort that require patience and a clear sense of what formative practice looks like. Efforts to improve assessment which don't follow this model risk becoming ineffective and burdensome. Similarly, assessment should be used to direct students to think and reflect upon performance, and lead to meaningful tasks that put feedback into action.

Assessment should focus on helping student to master the domain

Learning and exam performance are not mutually exclusive outcomes that educators must choose between. When rehearsing the final exam becomes the sole focus of education, it can lead to short-term improvements in performance at the expense of deeper and more effective forms of learning. In the long run, this reduces both the progress students can make, and their ability to perform well in assessment. Instead, teachers should choose assessment which helps students to learn the relevant academic domain in a systematic way, giving plenty of opportunities to deliberately practise the relevant skills and knowledge.

9.7 Summary

Putting assessment changes into practice is the hardest stage of all, so to ensure you are successful, make sure your goals are achievable, focused and measurable. Teachers need to remember that they cannot easily replicate the experimental design or controls of university researchers. Instead, their focus should be on 'disciplined enquiry' into the specific issues they have in their own institution. Disciplined enquiry means asking effective questions, choosing appropriate research on which to base change and following a systematic methodology.

To make the best use of the information contained in this book, you must build a bridge between the *how* and the *why* of assessment. Great knowledge cannot lead to great practice without both patience and reflection. The role of assessment is to facilitate reflection by giving us a sense of the impact our teaching is having. The role of the teacher is to reflect on learning and to seek to be better.

Exploring further

The best source for information on planning and managing assessment interventions is the Education Endowment Foundation (https://educationendowmentfoundation.org.uk/), who offer a host of resources on disciplined enquiry in schools. Their *DIY Evaluation Toolkit* will talk you through the process of planning and evaluating an intervention.

- Education Endowment Foundation (2017a) *DIY Evaluation Guide*. [online] Available at: https://educationendowmentfoundation.org.uk/resources/diy-guide/getting-started

References

Antoniou, P and James, M (2014) Exploring Formative Assessment in Primary School Classrooms: Developing a Framework of Actions and Strategies. *Educational Assessment, Evaluation and Accountability*, 26(2): 153–76.

Assessment Reform Group (1999) *Assessment for Learning: Beyond the Black Box*. Cambridge: Assessment Reform Group.

Baird, J, Hopfenbeck, T, Newton, P, Stobart, G and Steen-Utheim, A (2014) *State of the Field Review: Assessment and Learning*. Oslo: Norwegian Knowledge Centre for Education.

Baird, J-A, Andrich, D, Hopfenbeck, T N and Stobart, G (2017) Assessment and Learning: Fields Apart? *Assessment in Education: Principles, Policy & Practice*, 24(3): 317–50.

Baltzer, K and Colardyn, D (2006) *Improving Teaching and Learning for Adults with Basic Skill Needs through Formative Assessment: Case Study Denmark*. Paris: OECD Publishing.

Bangert-Drowns, R L, Kulik, C-L C, Kulik, J A and Morgan, M (1991) The Instructional Effect of Feedback in Test-like Events. *Review of Educational Research*, 61(2): 213–38.

Barron, B and Darling-Hammond, L (2008) *Teaching for Meaningful Learning: A Review of Research on Inquiry-Based and Cooperative Learning*. Book Excerpt. George Lucas Educational Foundation.

Bell, B and Cowie, B (2001a) The Characteristics of Formative Assessment in Science Education. *Science Education*, 85: 536–53.

Bell, B and Cowie, B (2001b) Teacher Development for Formative Assessment. *Waikato Journal of Education*, 7: 37–49.

Bell, S (2010) Project-Based Learning for the 21st Century: Skills for the Future. *The Clearing House: A Journal of Educational Strategies, Issues and Ideas*, 83(2): 39–43.

Bennett, R E (2009) Formative Assessment: Can the Claims for Effectiveness Be Substantiated? in *Proceedings of the 35th Annual Meeting of the International Association for Educational Assessment – Assessment for a Creative World*. Brisbane, Australia, Sept. 2009. Brisbane: International Association for Educational Assessment.

Bennett, R E (2011) Formative Assessment: A Critical Review. *Assessment in Education: Principles, Policy & Practice*, 18(1): 5–25.

Bereiter, C and Scardamalia, M (1998) Beyond Bloom's Taxonomy: Rethinking Knowledge for the Knowledge Age, in Hargreaves, A, Lieberman, A, Fullen, M and Hopkins, D (eds) *International Handbook of Educational Change*. Dordrecht: Kluwer Academic, pp 675–92.

van den Berg, M, Harskamp, E G and Suhre, C J M (2016) Developing Classroom Formative Assessment in Dutch Primary Mathematics Education. *Educational Studies*, 42(4): 305–22.

Bjork, E L and Bjork, R A (2011) Making Things Hard on Yourself, but in a Good Way: Creating Desirable Difficulties to Enhance Learning. *Psychology and the Real World: Essays Illustrating Fundamental Contributions to Society*. New York: Worth Publishers, pp 56–64.

Bjork, R A (1994) Institutional Impediments to Effective Training *Learning, Remembering, Believing: Enhancing Human Performance*: 295–306.

Bjork, R A, Dunlosky, J and Kornell, N (2013) Self-regulated Learning: Beliefs, Techniques, and Illusions. *Annual Review of Psychology*, 64: 417–44.

Black, P and Wiliam, D (1998a) Assessment and Classroom Learning. *Assessment in Education: Principles, Policy & Practice*, 5(1): 7–74.

Black, P and Wiliam, D (1998b) Inside the Black Box: Raising Standards Through Classroom Assessment. *Phi Delta Kappan*, 80(2): 139–48.

Black, P and Wiliam, D (2003) 'In Praise of Educational Research': Formative Assessment. *British Educational Research Journal*, 29(5): 623–37.

Black, P and Wiliam, D (2005) Changing Teaching Through Formative Assessment: Research and Practice, in *Formative Assessment: Improving Learning in Secondary Classrooms*. Paris: OECD, pp 223–40.

Black, P, Harrison, C, Lee, C, Marshall, B and Wiliam, D (2003) The Nature of Value of Formative Assessment for Learning. *Improving Schools*, 6: 7–22.

Black, P, Harrison, C and Lee, C (2004) *Working Inside the Black Box: Assessment for Learning in the Classroom*. London: Granada Learning.

Bloom, B S (1956) *Taxonomy of Educational Objectives. Vol. 1: Cognitive Domain*. New York: McKay, pp 20–24.

Broadfoot, P M, Daugherty, R, Gardner, J, Gipps, C V, Harlen, W, James, M and Stobart, G (1999) *Assessment for Learning: Beyond the Black Box*. Cambridge, UK: University of Cambridge School of Education.

Brown, P C, Roediger, H L and Mcdaniel, M A (2014) *Make It Stick: The Science of Successful Learning.* Cambridge, MA: Harvard University Press.

Buchanan, T (2000) The Efficacy of a World-Wide Web Mediated Formative Assessment. *Journal of Computer Assisted Learning*, 16(3): 193–200.

Butler, A C, Fazio, L K and Marsh, E J (2011) The Hypercorrection Effect Persists Over a Week, but High-confidence Errors Return. *Psychonomic Bulletin & Review*, 18(6): 1238–44.

Butler, D L and Winne, P H (1995) Feedback and Self-regulated Learning: A Theoretical Synthesis. *Review of Educational Research*, 65(3): 245–81.

Butler, R (1988) Enhancing and Undermining Intrinsic Motivation: The Effects of Task Involving and Ego Involving Evaluation on Interest and Performance. *British Journal of Educational Psychology*, 58(1): 1–14.

Butler, R (2006) Are Mastery and Ability Goals both Adaptive? Evaluation, Initial Goal Construction and the Quality of Task Engagement. *British Journal of Educational Psychology*, 76(3): 595–611.

Capon, N and Kuhn, D (2004) What's So Good about Problem-based Learning? *Cognition and Instruction*, 22(1): 61–79.

Carter, A (2015) C*arter Review of Initial Teacher Training* (ITT). London: DfE.

Cartwright, K B (2012) Insights from Cognitive Neuroscience: The Importance of Executive Function for Early Reading Development and Education. *Early Education and Development*, 23(1): 24–36.

Cartwright, N and Hardie, J (2012) *Evidence based Policy: A Practical Guide to Doing It Better.* Oxford: Oxford University Press.

Center on the Developing Child at Harvard University (2017) E*xecutive Function & Self-Regulation.* Center on the Developing Child at Harvard University. [online] Available at: http://developingchild.harvard.edu/science/key-concepts/executive-function/ (accessed 19 December 2017).

Cepeda, N J, Pashler, H, Vul, E, Wixted, J T and Rohrer, D (2006) Distributed Practice in Verbal Recall Tasks: A Review and Quantitative Synthesis. *Psychological Bulletin*, 132(3): 354–80.

Cepeda, N J, Coburn, N, Rohrer, D, Wixted, J T, Mozer, M C and Pashler, H (2009) Optimizing Distributed Practice: Theoretical Analysis and Practical Implications. *Experimental Psychology*, 56(4): 236–46.

Chen, F and Andrade, H (2016) The Impact of Criteria-referenced Formative Assessment on Fifth-grade Students' Theater Arts Achievement. *The Journal of Educational Research*: 1–10.

Christodoulou, D (2017) *Making Good Progress? The Future of Assessment for Learning*. New ed. Oxford: Oxford Univeristy Press.

Coe, R (2012) The Nature of Educational Research – Exploring the Different Understandings of Educational Research, in Arthur, J, Waring, M, Coe, R and Hedges, L V (eds) *Research Methods and Methodologies in Education*. Thousand Oaks, CA: SAGE, pp 5–13.

Colliver, J A (2000) Effectiveness of Problem based Learning Curricula: Research and Theory. *Academic Medicine*, 75(3): 259–66.

Cook, J and Lewandowsky, S (2011) T*he Debunking Handbook*. [online] Available at: https://skepticalscience.com/docs/Debunking_Handbook.pdf.

Cordingley, P, Higgins, S, Greany, T, Buckler, N, Coles-Jordan, D, Crisp, B, Saunders, L and Coe, R (2015) *Developing Great Teaching: Lessons from the International Reviews into Effective Professional Development*. London: Teacher Development Trust.

Cornelissen, F, van Swet, J, Beijaard, D and Bergen, T (2011) Aspects of School–University Research Networks that Play a Role in Developing, Sharing and Using Knowledge Based on Teacher Research. *Teaching and Teacher Education*, 27(1): 147–56.

Cowie, B and Bell, B (1999) A Model of Formative Assessment in Science Education. *Assessment in Education: Principles, Policy & Practice*, 6(1): 101–16.

Crooks, T J (1988) The Impact of Classroom Evaluation Practices on Students. *Review of Educational Research*, 58(4): 438–81.

Davidson, N and Major, C H (2014) Boundary Crossings: Cooperative Learning, Collaborative Learning, and Problem-based Learning. *Journal on Excellence in College Teaching*, 25(3–4): 7–55.

De Luque, M F S and Sommer, S M (2000) The Impact of Culture on Feedback-seeking Behavior: An Integrated Model and Propositions. *Academy of Management Review*, 25(4): 829–49.

Deans for Impact (2016) *The Science of Learning*. [online] Available at: www.deansforimpact.org/wp-content/uploads/2016/12/The_Science_of_Learning.pdf (accessed 7 December 2017).

Debue, N and van de Leemput, C (2014) What Does Germane Load Mean? An Empirical Contribution to the Cognitive Load Theory. *Frontiers in Psychology*, 5: 1099.

Department for Education and Skills (2007) *Assessment for Learning 8 Schools Project Report*. [online] Available at: http://dera.ioe.ac.uk/7600/1/1f1ab286369a7-ee24df53c863a72da97-1.pdf (accessed 19 December 2017).

Didau, D and Rose, N (2016) *What Every Teacher Needs to Know about Psychology.* Melton, Woodbridge: John Catt Educational Ltd.

Dignath, C, Buettner, G and Langfeldt, H-P (2008) How Can Primary School Students Learn Self-regulated Learning Strategies Most Effectively?: A Meta-analysis on Self-Regulation Training Programmes. *Educational Research Review*, 3(2): 101–29.

D'Mello, S, Lehman, B, Pekrun, R and Graesser, A (2014) Confusion Can Be Beneficial for Learning. *Learning and Instruction*, 29: 153–70.

Dochy, F, Segers, M, Van den Bossche, P and Gijbels, D (2003) Effects of Problem-based Learning: A Meta-analysis. *Learning and Instruction*, 13(5): 533–68.

Dudai, Y (2004) The Neurobiology of Consolidations, or, How Stable is the Engram? *Annual Review of Psychology*, 55: 51–86.

Dunn, K E and Mulvenon, S W (2009) A Critical Review of Research on Formative Assessment: The Limited Scientific Evidence of the Impact of Formative Assessment in Education. *Practical Assessment, Research & Evaluation*, 14(7): 1–11.

Dyer, O (2016) Drill and Didactic Teaching Work Best, in Birbalsingh, K (ed) *Battle Hymn of the Tiger Teachers: The Michaela Way.* Melton, Woodbridge: John Catt Educational Ltd, pp 28–39.

Education Endowment Foundation (2017a) *DIY Evaluation Guide.* [online] Available at: https://educationendowmentfoundation.org.uk/resources/diy-guide/getting-started (accessed 4 July 2017).

Education Endowment Foundation (2017b) *Meta-cognition and Self-regulation – EEF Toolkit.* [online] Available at: https://educationendowmentfoundation.org.uk/resources/teaching-learning-toolkit/meta-cognition-and-self-regulation (accessed 19 December 2017).

Education Endowment Foundation (2017c) *Peer Tutoring | Toolkit Strand.* [online] Available at: https://educationendowmentfoundation.org.uk/resources/teaching-learning-toolkit/peer-tutoring (accessed 19 December 2017).

Ericsson, K A (2006) The Influence of Experience and Deliberate Practice on the Development of Superior Expert Performance. *The Cambridge Handbook of Expertise and Expert Performance*, 38: 685–705.

Ericsson, K A (2008) Deliberate Practice and Acquisition of Expert Performance: A General Overview. *Academic Emergency Medicine*, 15(11): 988–94.

Ericsson, K A (2016) *Peak: Secrets from the New Science of Expertise by K Anders Ericsson.* Boston, MA: Houghton Mifflin.

Falchikov, N and Goldfinch, J (2000) Student Peer Assessment in Higher

Education: A Meta-analysis Comparing Peer and Teacher Marks. *Review of Educational Research*, 70(3): 287–322.

Fitzgerald, L M, Arvaneh, M and Dockree, P M (2017) Domain-specific and Domain-general Processes Underlying Metacognitive Judgments. *Consciousness and Cognition*, 49: 264–77.

Fuchs, L S and Fuchs, D (1986) Effects of Systematic Formative Evaluation: A Meta-Analysis. *Exceptional Children*, 53(3): 199–208.

Galdin-O'Shea, H (2015) Leading 'Disciplined Enquiries' in Schools, in Brown, C (ed) *Leading the Use of Research and Evidence in Schools*. London: Institute of Education Press, pp 91–106.

Ginsburg-Block, M D, Rohrbeck, C A and Fantuzzo, J W (2006) A Meta-analytic Review of Social, Self-concept, and Behavioral Outcomes of Peer-assisted Learning. *Journal of Educational Psychology*, 98: 732–49.

Gladwell, M (2009) *Outliers: The Story of Success*. London: Penguin.

Goldacre, B (2013) *Building Evidence into Education*. London: DfE.

Hambrick, D Z, Altmann, E M, Oswald, F L, Meinz, E J and Gobet, F (2007) Facing Facts about Deliberate Practice. *Frontiers in Psychology*, 5: 751.

Hattie, J (2008) *Visible Learning: A Synthesis of over 800 Meta-analyses Relating to Achievement*. London: Routledge.

Hattie, J and Timperley, H (2007) The Power of Feedback. *Review of Educational Research*, 77(1): 81–112.

Hayward, L (2015) Assessment is Learning: The Preposition Vanishes. *Assessment in Education: Principles, Policy & Practice*, 22(1): 27–43.

Healy, A F, Kosslyn, S M and Shiffrin, R M (1992) *From Learning Processes to Cognitive Processes: Essays in Honor of William K. Estes*. Hillsdale, NJ: L. Erlbaum.

Heath, C and Heath, D (2011) *Switch: How to Change Things When Change Is Hard*. London: Random House Business.

Heitink, M C, Van der Kleij, F M, Veldkamp, B P, Schildkamp, K and Kippers, W B (2016) A Systematic Review of Prerequisites for Implementing Assessment for Learning in Classroom Practice. *Educational Research Review*, 17: 50–62.

Higton, J, Leonardi, S, Choudhoury, A, Richards, N, Owen, D and Sofroniou, N (2017) *Teacher Workload Survey 2016*. London: DfE.

Hintzman, D L and Rogers, M K (1973) Spacing Effects in Picture Memory. *Memory & Cognition*, 1(4): 430–34.

Hmelo, C E, Holton, D L and Kolodner, J L (2000) Designing to Learn about Complex Systems. *The Journal of the Learning Sciences*, 9(3): 247–98.

Hmelo-Silver, C E, Duncan, R G and Chinn, C A (2007) Scaffolding and Achievement in Problem-based and Inquiry Learning: A Response to Kirschner, Sweller, and Clark (2006). *Educational Psychologist*, 42(2): 99–107.

Hopfenbeck, T N and Stobart, G (2015) Large-scale Implementation of Assessment for Learning. *Assessment in Education: Principles, Policy & Practice*, 22(1): 1–2.

Hopfenbeck, T N, Flórez Petour, M T and Tolo, A (2015) Balancing Tensions in Educational Policy Reforms: Large-scale Implementation of Assessment for Learning in Norway. *Assessment in Education: Principles, Policy & Practice*, 22(1): 44–60.

Hursh, D (2007) Assessing No Child Left Behind and the Rise of Neoliberal Education Policies. *American Educational Research Journal*, 44(3): 493–518.

Hutchinson, C and Hayward, L (2005) The Journey So Far: Assessment for Learning in Scotland. *Curriculum Journal*, 16(2): 225–48.

Jacob, R and Parkinson, J (2015) The Potential for School-based Interventions that Target Executive Function to Improve Academic Achievement: A Review. *Review of Educational Research*, 85(4): 512–52.

Johnson, D W, Johnson, R T and Smith, K A (2006) *Active Learning: Cooperation in the College Classroom.* Edina, MN: Interaction Book Co.

Johnson, D W, Johnson, R T and Smith, K A (2014) Cooperative Learning: Improving University Instruction by Basing Practice on Validated Theory. *Journal on Excellence in University Teaching*, 25(4): 1–26.

Johnson, D W, Johnson, R T and Stanne, M B (2000) *Cooperative Learning Methods: A Meta-analysis.* Minneapolis, MN: University of Minnesota

Jonsson, A, Lundahl, C and Holmgren, A (2015) Evaluating a Large-scale Implementation of Assessment for Learning in Sweden. *Assessment in Education: Principles, Policy & Practice*, 22(1): 104–21.

Karpicke, J D and Bauernschmidt, A (2011) Spaced Retrieval: Absolute Spacing Enhances Learning Regardless of Relative Spacing. *Journal of Experimental Psychology: Learning, Memory, and Cognition*, 37(5): 1250–57.

Karpicke, J D and Blunt, J R (2011) Retrieval Practice Produces More Learning than Elaborative Studying with Concept Mapping. *Science*, 331(6018): 772–75.

Karpicke, J D and Roediger III, HL (2007) Expanding Retrieval Practice Promotes Short-term Retention, but Equally Spaced Retrieval Enhances Long-term Retention. *Journal of Experimental Psychology: Learning, Memory, and Cognition*, 33(4): 704–19.

Karpicke, J D and Roediger, H L (2008) The Critical Importance of Retrieval for Learning. *Science*, 319(5865): 966–68.

Karpicke, J D, Butler, A C and Roediger III, HL (2009) Metacognitive Strategies in Student Learning: Do Students Practise Retrieval When They Study on Their Own? *Memory*, 17(4): 471–79.

Kelly, A V (2004) *The Curriculum: Theory and Practice*. 6th ed. London: SAGE.

Killian, S (2017) *Hattie Effect Size 2016 Update*. The Australian Society for Evidence Based Teaching. [online] Available at: www.evidencebasedteaching. org.au/hattie-effect-size-2016-update/ (accessed 19 December 2017).

Kingston, N and Nash, B (2011) Formative Assessment: A Meta-analysis and a Call for Research. *Educational Measurement: Issues and Practice*, 30(4): 28–37.

Kirby, J (2016) Homework as Revision, in Birbalsingh, K (ed) *Battle Hymn of the Tiger Teachers: The Michaela Way*. Melton, Woodbridge: John Catt Educational Ltd, pp 54–66.

Kirschner, F, Paas, F and Kirschner, P A (2009) A Cognitive Load Approach to Collaborative Learning: United Brains for Complex Tasks. *Educational Psychology Review*, 21(1): 31–42.

Kirschner, P A (2002) Cognitive Load Theory: Implications of Cognitive Load Theory on the Design of Learning. *Learning and Instruction*, 12(1): 1–10.

Kirschner, P A, Sweller, J and Clark, R E (2006) Why Minimal Guidance During Instruction Does Not Work: An Analysis of the Failure of Constructivist, Discovery, Problem-based, Experiential, and Inquiry-based Teaching. *Educational Psychologist*, 41(2): 75–86.

Kluger, A N and DeNisi, A (1996) The Effects of Feedback Interventions on Performance: A Historical Review, a Meta-analysis, and a Preliminary Feedback Intervention Theory. *Psychological Bulletin*, 119(2): 254–84.

Kluger, A N and Nir, D (2006) Feedforward First – Feedback Later. *26th International Conference of Applied Psychology*. Athens, Greece.

Kulhavy, R W and Stock, W A (1989) Feedback in Written Instruction: The Place of Response Certitude. *Educational Psychology Review*, 1(4): 279–308.

Kuo, F and Chiang, H (2015) Story Animation: Helping Students Build Connections Between Words and Pictures in Multimedia Learning. International Conference on English Instruction and Assessment. [online] Available at http://fllcccu.ccu.edu.tw/conference/2005conference_2/download C (accessed 19 December 2017).

Laal, M, Geranpaye, L and Daemi, M (2013) Individual Accountability in Collaborative Learning. *Procedia-Social and Behavioral Sciences*, 93: 286–89.

Lai, E R (2011) *Metacognition: A Literature Review.* Always Learning: Pearson research report. [online] Available at: http://images.pearsonassessments. com/images/tmrs/metacognition_literature_review_final.pdf (accessed 19 December 2017).

Lange, C, Costley, J and Han, S L (2016) Informal Cooperative Learning in Small Groups: The Effect of Scaffolding on Participation. *Issues in Educational Research*, 26(2): 260–79.

Lee, C and Wiliam, D (2005) Studying Changes in the Practice of Two Teachers Developing Assessment for Learning. *Teacher Development*, 9(2): 265–83.

Lee, T D and Genovese, E D (1988) Distribution of Practice in Motor Skill Acquisition: Learning and Performance Effects Reconsidered. *Research Quarterly for Exercise and Sport*, 59(4): 277–87.

Leong, W S and Tan, K (2014) What (More) Can, and Should, Assessment Do for Learning? Observations from 'Successful Learning Context' in Singapore. *The Curriculum Journal*, 25(4): 593–619.

Lepper, M R, Drake, M F and O'Donnell-Johnson, T (1997) Scaffolding Techniques of Expert Human Tutors, in Hogan, K and Pressley, M (eds) *Advances in Learning & Teaching. Scaffolding Student Learning: Instructional Approaches and Issues.* Cambridge, MA: Brookline Books, pp 108–44.

Lim, E P and Tan, A (1999) Educational Assessment in Singapore. *Assessment in Education: Principles, Policy & Practice*, 6(3): 391–404.

Liu, N-F and Carless, D (2006) Peer Feedback: The Learning Element of Peer Assessment. *Teaching in Higher Education*, 11(3): 279–90.

Lloyd, C, Edovald, T, Kiss, Z, Morris, S, Skipp, A and Ahmed, H (2015) *Paired Reading – Evaluation Report and Executive Summary.* Education Endowment Foundation. [online] Available at: https://educationendowmentfoundation.org. uk/public/files/Projects/Evaluation_Reports/Peer_Tutoring_in_Secondary_ Schools.pdf (accessed 19 December 2017).

Loyens, S M, Kirschner, P and Paas, F (2011) Problem-based Learning, in Harris, K R, Graham, S and Urdan, T (eds) *APA Educational Psychology Handbook*. Washington, DC: American Psychological Association.

Macnamara, B N, Hambrick, D Z and Oswald, F L (2014) Deliberate Practice and Performance in Music, Games, Sports, Education, and Professions: A Meta-analysis. *Psychological Science*, 25(8): 1608–18.

Mannion, J and Mercer, N (2016) Learning to Learn: Improving Attainment, Closing the Gap at Key Stage 3. *The Curriculum Journal*, 27(2): 246–71.

Mayer, R E (2002) *The Promise of Educational Psychology: Teaching for Meaningful Learning.* London: Prentice Hall.

Mayer, R E and Anderson, R B (1991) Animations Need Narrations: An Experimental Test of a Dual-coding Hypothesis. *Journal of Educational Psychology*, 83(4): 484–90.

McDougall, D, Saunders, W and Goldenberg, C (2007) Inside the Black Box of School Reform: Explaining the How and Why of Change at Getting Results Schools. *International Journal of Disability, Development and Education*, 54(1): 51–89.

McLaughlin, C, McIntyre, D and Black-Hawkins, C (2006) *Researching Teachers, Researching Schools, Researching Networks: A Review of the Literature.* Cambridge: University of Cambridge.

McMaster, K L, Fuchs, D and Fuchs, L S (2006) Research on Peer-assisted Learning Strategies: The Promise and Limitations of Peer-mediated Instruction. *Reading & Writing Quarterly*, 22(1): 5–25.

Menzies, V, Hewitt, C, Kokotsaki, D, Collyer, C and Wiggins, A (2016) *Project Based Learning – Evaluation Report and Executive Summary.* Education Endowment Foundation. [online] Available at: https://educationendowmentfoundation.org.uk/public/files/Projects/Evaluation_Reports/EEF_Project_Report_Project_Based_Learning.pdf (accessed 19 December 2017).

Metcalfe, J and Finn, B (2012) Hypercorrection of High Confidence Errors in Children. *Learning and Instruction*, 22(4): 253–61.

Moore, D S (1982) Reconsidering Bloom's Taxonomy of Educational Objectives, Cognitive Domain. *Educational Theory*, 32(1): 29–34.

Morgan, J C (1994) *Individual Accountability in Cooperative Learning Groups: Its Impact on Achievement and on Attitude with Grade Three Students.* Unpublished Master's thesis, University of Manitoba.

Mullaney, K M, Carpenter, S K, Grotenhuis, C and Burianek, S (2014) Waiting for Feedback Helps if You Want to Know the Answer: The Role of Curiosity in the Delay-of-feedback Benefit. *Memory & Cognition*, 42(8): 1273–84.

Mullet, H G, Butler, A C, Verdin, B, von Borries, R and Marsh, E J (2014) Delaying Feedback Promotes Transfer of Knowledge Despite Student Preferences to Receive Feedback Immediately. *Journal of Applied Research in Memory and Cognition*, 3(3): 222–29.

Narciss, S and Huth, K (2004) How to Design Informative Tutoring Feedback for Multimedia Learning, in Niegemann, H M and Leutner, D (eds) *Instructional Design for Multimedia Learning.* Münster: Waxmann, pp 181–95.

Natriello, G (1987) The Impact of Evaluation Processes on Students. *Educational Psychologist*, 22(2): 155–75.

Nelson, M M and Schunn, C D (2009a) The Nature of Feedback: How Different Types of Peer Feedback Affect Writing Performance. *Instructional Science*, 37(4): 375–401.

Nelson, M M and Schunn, C D (2009b) The Nature of Feedback: How Different Types of Peer Feedback Affect Writing Performance. *Instructional Science*, 37(4): 375–401.

Neuenhaus, N, Artelt, C, Lingel, K and Schneider, W (2011) Fifth Graders Metacognitive Knowledge: General or Domain-specific? *European Journal of Psychology of Education*, 26(2): 163–78.

Nicol, D J and Macfarlane Dick, D (2006) Formative Assessment and Self-regulated Learning: A Model and Seven Principles of Good Feedback Practice. *Studies in Higher Education*, 31(2): 199–218.

Nuttall, D L (ed) (1986) Assessment for Learning, in Nuttall, D L (ed) *Assessing Educational Achievement*. London ; Philadelphia: Falmer Press Ltd, pp 7–18.

Nyhan, B and Reifler, J (2010) When Corrections Fail: The Persistence of Political Misperceptions. *Political Behavior*, 32(2): 303–30.

Ofsted (2008) *Assessment for Learning: The Impact of National Strategy Support*. [online] Available at: http://dera.ioe.ac.uk/9309/1/Assessment%20for%20 learning%20-%20the%20impact%20of%20National%20Strategy%20support.pdf (accessed 19 December 2017).

Olina, Z and Sullivan, H J (2002) Effects of Classroom Evaluation Strategies on Student Achievement and Attitudes. *Educational Technology Research and Development*, 50(3): 61–75.

Opitz, B, Ferdinand, N K and Mecklinger, A (2011) Timing Matters: The Impact of Immediate and Delayed Feedback on Artificial Language Learning. *Frontiers in Human Neuroscience*, 5: 8.

Organisation for Economic Co-operation and Development (2005) *Formative Assessment: Improving Learning in Secondary Classrooms*. Paris: OECD Publishing.

Paas, F, Renkl, A and Sweller, J (2003) Cognitive Load Theory and Instructional Design: Recent Developments. *Educational Psychologist*, 38(1): 1–4.

Pashler, H, Rohrer, D, Cepeda, N J and Carpenter, S K (2007) Enhancing Learning and Retarding Forgetting: Choices and Consequences. *Psychonomic Bulletin & Review*, 14(2): 187–93.

Pekrun, R, Cusack, A, Murayama, K, Elliot, A J and Thomas, K (2014) The Power of Anticipated Feedback: Effects on Students' Achievement Goals and Achievement Emotions. *Learning and Instruction*, 29(Supplement C): 115–24.

Pellegrino, J W (2002) Knowing What Students Know. *Issues in Science and Technology*, 19(2): 48–52.

Pellegrino, J W, Glaser, R and Chudowsky, N (eds) (2001) *Knowing What Students Know: The Science and Design of Educational Assessment*. Washington, DC: National Academies Press.

Plass, J L, Moreno, R and Brünken, R (2010) *Cognitive Load Theory*. New York: Cambridge University Press.

Pollard, A and Triggs, P (2001) *What Pupils Say: Changing Policy and Practice in Primary Education*. London/New York: Continuum.

Pollitt, A (2012) Comparative Judgement for Assessment. *International Journal of Technology and Design Education*, 22(2): 157–70.

Popham, W J (2008) *Transformative Assessment*. Alexandria, VA: Association for Supervision & Curriculum Development.

Popham, W J (2011) *Transformative Assessment in Action: An Inside Look at Applying the Process*. Alexandria, VA: Association for Supervision & Curriculum Development.

Pratt, N (2016) Neoliberalism and the (Internal) Marketisation of Primary School Assessment in England. *British Educational Research Journal*, 42(5): 890–905.

Prince, M (2004) Does Active Learning Work? A Review of the Research. *Journal of Engineering Education*, 93(3): 223–31.

Puntambekar, S and Hubscher, R (2005) Tools for Scaffolding Students in a Complex Learning Environment: What Have We Gained and What Have We Missed? *Educational Psychologist*, 40(1): 1–12.

Ratnam-Lim, C T L and Tan, K H K (2015) Large-scale Implementation of Formative Assessment Practices in an Examination-oriented Culture. *Assessment in Education: Principles, Policy & Practice*, 22(1): 61–78.

Reiser, B J (2004) Scaffolding Complex Learning: The Mechanisms of Structuring and Problematizing Student Work. *The Journal of the Learning Sciences*, 13(3): 273–304.

Roediger, H L and Butler, A C (2011) The Critical Role of Retrieval Practice in Long-term Retention. *Trends in Cognitive Sciences*, 15(1): 20–27.

Rohrbeck, C A, Ginsburg-Block, M D, Fantuzzo, J W and Miller, T R (2003) Peer-assisted Learning Interventions with Elementary School Students: A Meta-analytic Review. *Journal of Educational Psychology*, 95(2), 240–57.

Rosenshine, B (2012) Principles of Instruction: Research-Based Strategies That All Teachers Should Know. *American Educator*, 36(1): 12–19.

Rosenshine, B and Meister, C (1994) Reciprocal Teaching: A Review of the Research. *Review of Educational Research*, 64(4): 479–530.

Ruiz-Primo, M and Furtak, E M (2006) Informal formative assessment and scientific inquiry: Exploring teachers' practices and student learning. *Educational Assessment*, 11(3–4): 237–63.

Schneider, M and Preckel, F (2017) Variables Associated with Achievement in Higher Education: A Systematic Review of Meta-analyses. *Psychological Bulletin*, 143(6): 565–600.

Schraw, G, Crippen, K J and Hartley, K (2006) Promoting Self-regulation in Science Education: Metacognition as Part of a Broader Perspective on Learning. *Research in Science Education*, 36(1–2): 111–39.

Scott, B M and Berman, A F (2013) Examining the Domain-specificity of Metacognition Using Academic Domains and Task-specific Individual Differences. *Australian Journal of Educational & Developmental Psychology*, 13: 28–43.

Scriven, M. (1967) The Methodology of Evaluation, in Tyler, R W, Gagné, R M and Scriven, M (eds) *Perspectives of Curriculum Evaluation*. Chicago, IL: Rand McNally, pp 39–83.

Shute, V J (2008) Focus on Formative Feedback. *Review of Educational Research*, 78(1): 153–89.

Smolen, P, Zhang, Y and Byrne, J H (2016) The Right Time to Learn: Mechanisms and Optimization of Spaced Learning. *Nature Reviews. Neuroscience*, 17(2): 77–88.

Snook, I, O'Neill, J, Clark, J, O'Neill, A-M and Openshaw, R (2009) Invisible Learnings? A Commentary on John Hattie's Book: Visible Learning: A synthesis of over 800 Meta-analyses Relating to Achievement. *New Zealand Journal of Educational Studies*, 44(1): 93–106.

Soderstrom, N C and Bjork, R A (2015) Learning Versus Performance: An Integrative Review. *Perspectives on Psychological Science*, 10(2): 176–99.

Springer, L, Stanne, M E and Donovan, S S (1999) Effects of Small-group Learning on Undergraduates in Science, Mathematics, Engineering, and Technology: A Meta-Analysis. *Review of Educational Research*, 69(1): 21–51.

Stewart, W (2015) Think You've Implemented Assessment for Learning? *TES*. [online] Available at: www.tes.com/news/tes-archive/tes-publication/think-youve-implemented-assessment-learning (accessed 19 December 2017).

Stiggins, R J (2002) Assessment Crisis: The Absence of Assessment for Learning. *Phi Delta Kappan*, 83(10): 758–65.

Stiggins, R (2005) From Formative Assessment to Assessment for Learning: A Path to Success in Standards-based Schools. *Phi Delta Kappan*, 87(4): 324–28.

Stoll, L, Bolam, R, McMahon, A, Wallace, M and Thomas, S (2006) Professional Learning Communities: A Review of the Literature. *Journal of Educational Change*, 7(4): 221–58.

Strobel, J and van Barneveld, A (2009) When is PBL More Effective? A Meta-synthesis of Meta-analyses Comparing PBL to Conventional Classrooms. *Interdisciplinary Journal of Problem-based Learning*, 3(1): 44–58.

Sweller, J (1994) Cognitive Load Theory, Learning Difficulty, and Instructional Design. *Learning and Instruction*, 4(4): 295–312.

Taylor, C and Spence-Thomas K (2015) Understanding Impact and the Cycle of Enquiry. In *Leading the Use of Research and Evidence in Schools*. London: Institute of Education Press, pp 125–36.

Terhart, E (2011) Has John Hattie Really Found the Holy Grail of Research on Teaching? An Extended Review of Visible Learning. *Journal of Curriculum Studies*, 43(3): 425–38.

Thompson, M, Goe, L, Paek, P and Ponte, E (2004) *Study of the California Formative Assessment and Support System for Teachers: Relationship of BTSA/CFASST and Student Achievement*. Princeton: Educational Testing Service.

Tigelaar, D E H and Beijaard, D (eds) (2015) *Formative Assessments and Teacher Professional Learning*. London: Routledge.

Topping, K J (2005) Trends in Peer Learning. *Educational Psychology*, 25(6): 631–45.

Van Boxtel, C, Van der Linden, J and Kanselaar, G (2000) Collaborative Learning Tasks and the Elaboration of Conceptual Knowledge. *Learning and Instruction*, 10(4): 311–30.

Van Loon, M H, Dunlosky, J, Van Gog, T, Van Merriënboer, J J and De Bruin, A B (2015) Refutations in Science Texts Lead to Hypercorrection of Misconceptions Held with High Confidence. *Contemporary Educational Psychology*, 42: 39–48.

Veenman, M V, Van Hout-Wolters, B H and Afflerbach, P (2006) Metacognition and Learning: Conceptual and Methodological Considerations. *Metacognition and Learning*, 1(1): 3–14.

Vescio, V, Ross, D and Adams, A (2008) A Review of Research on the Impact of Professional Learning Communities on Teaching Practice and Student Learning. *Teaching and Teacher Education*, 24(1): 80–91.

Voogt, J and Kasurinen, H (2005) Finland: Emphasising Development Instead of Competition and Comparison, in Looney, J. (ed) *Formative Assessment: Improving Learning in Secondary Classrooms*. Paris: OECD, pp 149–56.

White, B Y and Frederiksen, J R (1998) Inquiry, Modeling, and Metacognition: Making Science Accessible to all Students. *Cognition and Instruction*, 16(1): 3–118.

Wiliam, D (1998) The Validity of Teachers' Assessments. *22nd Annual Conference of the International Group for the Psychology of Mathematics Education*. Stellenbosch, South Africa.

Wiliam, D (2009) *Assessment for Learning: Why, What and How?* London: Cambridge Assessment Network: Institute of Education, University of London, pp 1–13.

Wiliam, D (2011) *Embedded Formative Assessment*. Bloomington, IN: Solution Tree Press.

Wiliam, D (2013) Assessment: The Bridge Between Teaching and Learning. *Voices from the Middle*, 21(2): 15–20.

Wiliam, D (2014) Why Teaching Will Never Be a Research-based Profession and Why That's a Good Thing. *ResearchEd National Conference*. Raine's Foundation School, London.

Wiliam, D (2016) *Leadership for Teacher Learning: Creating a Culture Where All Teachers Improve So That All Students Succeed*. West Palm Beach, FL: Learning Sciences International.

Wiliam, D (2017) Learning and Assessment: A Long and Winding Road? *Assessment in Education: Principles, Policy & Practice*, 24(3): 309–16.

Wiliam, D and Thompson, M (2008) Integrating Assessment with Instruction: What Will It Take to Make It Work? in Dwyer, C A (ed) *The Future of Assessment: Shaping Teaching and Learning*. New York: Lawrence Erlbaum Associates, pp 53–82.

Wiliam, D, Lee, C, Harrison, C and Black, P (2004) Teachers Developing Assessment for Learning: Impact on Student Achievement. *Assessment in Education: Principles, Policy & Practice*, 11(1): 49–65.

Williams, R L, Carroll, E and Hautau, B (2005) Individual Accountability in Cooperative Learning Groups at the College Level: Differential Effects on High, Average, and Low Exam Performers. *Journal of Behavioral Education*, 14(3): 167–88.

Willingham, D T (2006) How Knowledge Helps. *American Federation of Teachers*. [online] Available at: www.aft.org/periodical/american-educator/spring-2006/how-knowledge-helps (accessed 19 December 2017).

Willingham, D T (2010) *Why Don't Students Like School? A Cognitive Scientist Answers Questions about How the Mind Works and What it Means for the Classroom*. 1st ed. San Francisco, CA: Jossey Bass.

Wininger, S R (2005) Using Your Tests to Teach: Formative Summative Assessment. *Teaching of Psychology*, 32(3): 164–66.

Yin, Y, Tomita, M K and Shavelson, R J (2014) Using Formal Embedded Formative Assessments Aligned with a Short-term Learning Progression to Promote Conceptual Change and Achievement in Science. *International Journal of Science Education*, 36(4): 531–52.

Index